# THE ART OF DARKNESS

# The Art of Darkness

David McFadden

McClelland and Stewart

*The Canadian Publishers*
McClelland and Stewart Limited
25 Hollinger Road, Toronto M4B 3G2

*Canadian Cataloguing in Publication Data*

McFadden, David, 1940-
    The art of darkness

Poems.
ISBN 0-7710-5512-9

I. Title.

PS8525.F32A77 1984    C811'.54    C84-098770-6
PR9199.3.M243A77 1984

The publisher makes grateful acknowledgment to the Ontario
Arts Council and the Canada Council for their assistance.

Set in Sabon by Coach House Press.
Printed and bound in Canada by Gagné Ltd.

As there comes light from heaven, and words from breath....
— *Measure for Measure*

It was widely rumoured that certain persons had heard celestial music coming down from heaven around two o'clock in the morning on New Year's Day. And they say it has been heard every eighth day since.... I found myself intrigued, and invited a group of friends to come to my humble cottage on the nineteenth day of March. We all listened intently, from early evening on, but we heard nothing until the first sunbeams touched the far end of the eastern sky. Then all at once we heard a voice — we heard music — coming from the plum tree near my window.
— Issa

Only a little man, one of those emasculated dancers who suddenly spring up from behind bottles of white brandy, said sarcastically in a very low voice: "Viva Paris!", as if to say: "Here we do not care for ability, technique or mastery. Here we care for something else."
— Lorca

# Contents

# Preface

It's been a wonderful summer but now the dead leaves are blowing through the streets of Toronto like old poems and the weary poet, lacking enthusiasm but striving for faith, goes through his manuscript for the last time, changing a comma here and wishing he hadn't used the word "heart" quite so often but saying it's too late to do anything about it now. "I turned on the furnace in my house today," someone is saying in the next room. The word "heart" is used more than a hundred times in this book; it's a symbol, I suppose, of the purity and perfection we sense at the centre of everything, in spite of everything. The heart is the hearth of the world, the underlying lava that occasionally erupts and burns the way clear for fresh innocence.

Something should be said about some of these poems. "Country of the Open Heart," "Night of Endless Radiance" and "Stormy January" were written with the help of the I Ching, the ancient Book of Changes. "A New Romance," published as a book by Cross Country Press in Montreal in 1979 and not included here, is part of that series. The compositional process involves the metaphorical cutting and stretching of a canvas in total darkness. Coins are tossed for a number that will represent the number of parts of the projected poem, coins are tossed to determine the number of lines in each part, then the writing begins and everything that is in the air goes into the poem. Revision is endless, or threatens to be. The urge is there to continue revising until nothing is left of the first draft but the basic formal shape: all the "hearts" disappear eventually, go back into the air from which they came. Fresh innocence wants to make a map of the moment but since the map takes so long to draw the moment becomes decidedly imaginary. One doesn't want to make this seem more serious than the arms talks but perhaps it is, as the lava might say if it could talk and maybe it can, and does. It's a strange way of writing but I love it: the words are born and die like individual cells of the body and only the form is divine.

Then there are the poisonous poems: "Pinnochio" (my favourite), "Greaseball," "The Rat," "Kitsilano Beach" and so on. I enjoyed writing these poems and thought I understood them at the time but when I looked back at them a year or two later they became shockingly transparent and I understood them in new ways, as dreams representing sub-surface currents in my life at the time, currents I knew nothing about. Analysis of these poems is strictly forbidden. One seldom knows if one is operating in the personal or the collective mode, at least not until the operation is completed and the scar has healed. Anything but total absorption in the insanities of the surface seems cowardly, as I wish I'd had the wit to say to a student at the University of Western Ontario recently. She'd just finished reading *A Trip around Lake Erie* and said: "What are we supposed to get out of this book? It seems so superficial. It's not at all like *Paradise Lost*." Well, I'm a nice man and have been blessed by wonderful friends who are intelligent enough to be wary of nice men. The crew of the *Enola Gay* were nice men. I talked to God once and he seemed nice too.

The title of this book comes from a line in "Night of Endless Radiance" and refers to that Conradian Africa where we all dwell today, inescapably, every tree full of corpses. At first I thought it referred to some kind of Conradian Africa within, but now I see it refers to our current global dilemma, in which each of us has to live with no light but the light of our own individuality and courage. It refers to our enormous collective darkness, a darkness hitherto not part of human experience, a darkness in which each of us is trapped like a Jew on the eve of the Holocaust, trapped in a vision of this holy planet as a lifeless cinder. It would be a mistake to blame our collective darkness on the hoodlums who run the arms race, for who are they but we? Courage has always been required but never has it been so difficult to muster.

It's an individual problem and there are no formulae for courage, but inspiration can perhaps be derived from the archetypal image of the artist as one who has forsaken illusions and is forced to operate in a field of total darkness, one who feels irresistibly compelled to try to fly where no one else has walked, armed only with the tiny flash of the heart (there's that word again), one who feels called upon to assume the role of some kind of agent of renewal, one who knows there is nothing new but that which can be made new by summoning the totality of human imagination and intelligence into the tiny globe of the skull, and one who always has to be awake and on the rack even while sensing the razorish truth in Carl Jung's 1946 comment to the effect that in the psyche of the artist and intellectual, "The brighter the light, the darker the shadow."

As a title, *The Art of Darkness* refers to that "rocking delight" Rilke speaks of, that earnest gathering of "depth and strength for the song of some coming poet, who will arise to speak of ecstasies beyond telling." Love isn't all but it must take precedence over all, no matter how difficult, fraught with indignities, embarrassing and unfashionable it may be. Now as never before it's our civic duty as citizens of the world to subject ourselves to ecstasy, to go beyond and discover the new oceans of ecstasy that lie waiting for the pure pilgrims of love, and to return and talk about it indiscriminately, passionately, like a fundamentalist door-knocker. To quote Jung again, "One is always in the dark about one's own personality. One needs others to get to know oneself."

As for the poems in this book, many editors and friends and even strangers have listened to and read many of them and have given me helpful comments. Many people have helped in many ways, more than they know in many cases. If you know who you are, thanks; if you don't, thanks too. I'm speaking of deep understanding, and a kind of rock-like compassion that goes far beyond commenting on the poems, and it's impossible even to think of acknowledging this sympathy adequately. One can only continue to be inspired by it.

# Night of Endless Radiance

## I

Night stares in at nature's abhorrent vacuum
and engulfs you again in your own absence
as you read your signature on each little cloud
and the world is drifting drifting drifting
across the face of the moon, a former lover,
vaguely remembering another ruined century
when Zen Buddhism was the wave of the future
as magic was the wave of the past, and soon
you'll be walking around town with your genitalia
exposed, for originality is nature's zipper and those
exposed are subject to rapid evolutionary change —
each image with its own little force field, invisible
until it strikes the fields of other images
like rays of light from stars viewed
by people on a train heading into the northern night
and the endless forest shudders with its own reality —
thought charged with unassuming power to enter and alter
the genetic code until you begin to resemble the thinker
whose thought you most admire — hence the notorious
Japanese reticence to show poetry to non-poets.

And one is often moved to think with emptiness,
not knowing what he or she is going to think,
for the night moves on familiar horseback
through the hoofbeats of ordinary life
stopping only to comfort the afflicted
and justify the ways of wealth to the rich
as if the heart which knows such fullness
couldn't bear to bare itself, and must hide
under fresh clouds of naked words unable to cope
with the nature of their unassuming power, and must protest
such fullness in a blinding flash of flesh, and must refuse
a moment's intimacy for fear of being overwhelmed
for there can be no ambition, no argument
in the face of a thinker thinking a thought.

And you can only hope God will dress up
and become visible like a bird or snake with long
eyelashes and tell you how wonderful you really are
but this is what you feel about The Night,
a mystical mansion afloat in a sea of blood,
a mind that bursts with loveliness when it thinks,
a mind aspiring to Nighthood, a mind
that can, at will, vanish, and reappear
thousands of miles away a moment later, so that one
can choose a mind at random and declare:
"This is what is must be to be The Night!"
For the light of illumination is not an earthly light,
is not a light that anyone can chart,
no sea of light, no gravity-bent sky of light,
no light that spills over mountains like pails of milk,
no light that grows like flowers on the sea,
no light that points at buried pots of gold,
no light that one can detect and track like wild beasts
or enemy ships in the radarless North Atlantic,
no ancient pots of light on ocean floors,
no lonely little light lost in a forest of light
and hoping to be discovered and made a star,
not even a spark that makes a turbine turn.
There is nothing abstract about this light, it is neither
electrical nor solar but can only be called
a radiant blackness, the radiance
of the mountains in the interior ignored
by the smug inhabitants of the coast,
a sudden turning up of diamonds
in the darkened cardgame of the unmined mind.
This is night's eternal radiance
which, in a moment's penetration, heals
forever the cancers of the modern soul
and plunges it into its own millennial adoration.
And there is only one test for true minds:
if they were to jump in the sea en masse
would dolphins save them
and with them on their Quasimodo shoulders
disappear in the moonless night
bound for Ancient Isles of Splendour?

## II

The night, the night, the milky night,
where does it end?
It spills over its own borders
until there is no trace of those borders
and not even the milky night itself silently
drunk with its own silent illumination
can remember where those borders were.
The stars are the night's stigmata.
Only the stars themselves in ordinary space
and the occasionally mysterious conflagration
shimmering briefly on illusory horizons
remind the night it is the night.

The night rides the earth like a knight
who has found a thousand holy grails
and stabs the heart of each pregnant sleeping
woman at the very moment she awakens.
The night is mad with its own desire
to continue being the night
for the night is so profoundly radiant
there is nothing else worth being
though there is always the danger of becoming,
or being mistaken for, the day.
The night does not know what day it is
nor has it any notion of its self-illumination.

The deaf shall inherit the night.

Miscellaneous crowds of apes swarm
in and out of the night like schools of dolphins
crossing imaginary equators, like disappointed saints
disowning their sainthood at the end of their lives,
and the night is a spider who has built a flawless web
in the fork of a branch about to be pruned, a night
where demons demonstrate their dire straights,
where pies are opened and birds fly out,
where πs are squared and thoughts fly out,
and darkness is another kind of light.
The night is all depth and no surface.
The night is a giant medicinal herb.

## III

The advantages and disadvantages of existence,
the development of the capacity to perceive
consciousness at first hand or even second,
whether to return groceries you've picked up
at the market by mistake and haven't paid for —
these aspects of the "argument with the self"
form the basis for the cellular hum that slips
in and out of consciousness like a mirage,
a metallic incrustation slipping in and out
of the Dewdney radar field and creating
a ghostly wind that has probably cancelled
by now your memory of having found this poem
under a carpet of moss and pine needles,
the ink running, the pages curling and discoloured,
the visual music speaking of a magnetic reality
where nothing exists that is not seen, where music
and obscure tactile sensations drift along
peripheral halls and through doors of déjà vu
and overwhelm you with their antique forms
and you open yourself to further dissolution
for you are a hunting animal and must find
each throbbing moment and destroy it
as in your sleep you sacrifice each dream
on the sacred altar of your tongue.

## IV

The advantages and disadvantages of having
a flower garden: how many rose petals would it take
to fill a mattress or smother a tiresome accordion player
who has been babbling on too long about your beloved
as if she were merely part of the dull murmur
bleeding under the world's fat linguistic veneer,
each cell in ceaseless argument with its neighbour,
each cell imprisoned in its own cell? Warden, treat
your cells well and you won't get cancer.
And the night bandits, instead of being captivated
by the beauty of your naked mind,

will be unable to resist your cellular cries of woe
and with their passkeys will infiltrate the cellblocks.
For your death is a breakdown of all that is dull
and even slightly predictable, another mysterious reality
where nothing exists that has not been set in wondrous rhyme.

And by now you are burning with enormous passion
and have forgiven the imperfections of this world,
your generosity causing electromagnetic waves of ecstasy
to break on the heavy hearts of unknown dreamers burdened
with the creation, preservation and destruction
of tiny intricate models of the universe. But art
isn't the sort of thing one speaks of in private.


V

An absence of music, not made
by blowing into brass tubes or hollow reeds,
an unforced absence, a vacuum strayed
from the myriad influence of surrounding music,
storming from the radiance
that separates each clod of earth
from a quietude of the heart, producing a music
too slippery to cling to or even to apprehend,
moves slowly along the Slocan Valley
and awakens the elk and deer with amorous touches
and causes men and women to become wobbly with desire,
the night a radiant mosaic of soft glories, the cities
of the eastern hemisphere all in flames.
Somewhere a wounded man is getting to his feet
randomly from a limited number of possibilities
and every dream he has ever dreamt is suddenly in his head
like a fire-line packed away in a fireproof box
at the end of a wooden wharf on a small lake surrounded
by endless forest five hundred miles north of Sioux Lookout,
a dash of red pepper pie in the sensational sky, dear reader.
And that man was you, John Keats. Look at this, a map
of Canada in the shape of a heart, the Great Lakes
little dimples full of tears and earnest restraint,
a country of the open heart where serenity is composed

line by total-lack-of-ambiguity line, perfect, perfect.
"This perfection has become overly elliptical,"
sang the Happy Twins as hand in hand they disappeared
over Sunset Hill, "and you'll never succeed in your search
for someone who will understand your naked mind
almost as well as you yourself understand it
on days when you almost understand it.
Everyone knows it's not easy for you
the way butter drips through the palm fronds,
gangs of midget bandits ignore you along the length
of night's passionate beach, Sappho decides to return
bearing streams of non-specific rainbow energies
and no one wants to hurt your pride by telling you
your dreams sound as if they were all invented."
You try to explain how so much depends upon
the way Miles Davis was playing in 1950 but no one listens
not even the whispering crowds of time travellers
masquerading as rosy velvet puffs of consciousness
in the middle of Service Station Nightmare.
"Only midgets have the intelligence to understand
this terrible public behaviour," they taunted,
and one velvet puff stepped forward, smiled, and asked
that his name, a famous one indeed, not be mentioned,
yet as he spoke it was obvious he was anticipating
the simplicity of his own unfettered ego, and when he said
he wanted everyone to know he'd be available
whenever needed and would do whatever was required,
one could sense a certain frivolity was mixed
with his desire to do battle with those who ignore
the soul-filled cries of the purest souls of any age.


VI


"These are the things they said to one another
under the rim of earth where Death is lord."
These are spells designed to enlighten the author
and these are messages written while on the road
and left behind to help him find the road again
when night has fallen and friends are few
and there is no room at the metaphor, nothing

but what you see in your everyday life.
And these are dreams seen in times of darkness,
private dreams becoming public and at play
with one's private views of public dreams,
dreams struggling to be free of convention
then abandoning the silly struggle to be perfect
and thereby becoming perfect as the sky is perfect
or as the world would be in the absence of those dreams,
the public mind struggling to create a private dream
and struggling to create the conditions of freedom
that would allow private dreams to find their own
perfection, for there is a turning point when the struggle
ends forever, a night of endless radiance.

But the night will always be haunted by a notion
that the morning will bring a return to an age
when everything everyone dreamt was as elegant
as the elaborate warnings Odysseus gave the suitors,
Odysseus the dreamer returned at last to find his heart's
desire being pulled to pieces by the modern age.
And what dreamer could you name who wouldn't be shocked
and reminded of a maddeningly purer existence
experienced in some ridiculous prenatal eternity
by the sight of a golden Thracian drinking vessel
bearing a daring pattern of negroid heads,
goat-headed snakes, acorns and armoured knights
appearing in her or his early afternoon mail?

And the tide goes in and out, civilizations
fall into the sea, and entire generations
are born grossly deformed, alienated forever
not from beauty and proportion but from a way
of being in which one can never be alienated
from beauty and proportion, and whatever action
the individual human being performs is full of
dreams and flawless unpremeditated grace.
Yet these are but the arts of peace, peace
that has so much in common with war, night
that has so much in common with radiant day,
for in either there is nothing more to do
than observe dreams with modest but mindless

respect — Alexander heeding his ancestor Herakles
calling him to the walls of Tyre —
a respect that moves through a world impossible
to understand, a moment impossible to understand,
yet filled with the power to create in the mind
the purity of the pre-dawn when the songs
of the forest birds and the cries of the sea birds
touch the soul like the lips of a beloved saint
and spasms convulse the floating heart
until it cannot hold back, it simply must
explode and fill the night with endless radiance
until even the Prince of Darkness is enlightened
and remains silent, unbreathing, overwhelmed
with grievous remorse, shocked at the cruel
stupidity of his life, his bones white hot
and radiant in their pockets of intelligent flesh,
his inner organs softly moaning with the joy
of enlightened existence: "All is forgiven."


# VII

— The old millpond reflected the flowering
horse chestnuts on a blue spring day
like an eye, a watery, slightly scum-covered
eye. And at night, after the fall of night,
when the eye blinked shut, the flowering
horse chestnuts could be seen playing chess.

At midnight the earth glowed with fabulous colour
and a pulse passed through the soft forest
as if the air had just become conscious
of the sadness of unknown gods and goddesses
at having to bar humanity from paradise.
It's for your own good, they cry.
Try to see things from our perspective
or, if you can't, from the perspective
of the glowing plasmic sadness
at the centre of the soul of the earth,
for the Incas of South America, it is said,
were massacred because they seemed so weird.

Yet it is time for instant coffee, and through
the window tiny green leaves of spring
are vibrating like furry rabbits mating in the wind.
She mentioned the Inca massacre in her suicide note.
She'd never developed the habit of closing her eyes
when she laughed, and as she laughed you'd have
the pleasure of seeing her staring at you
like a wild flower, for when the heart is opened
each beat is the charge of a velveteen bull
and what instinct will be left when the instinct
for beauty is finally extinct? The instinct of tyrants
trying to persuade you they have something worth hearing
when all they have to do is open their hearts
and in their speech you'll find snake-like figures
at the great doorway of heaven bidding you enter!
And so you enter! And suddenly you are back on earth
at midnight, the countryside glowing with fabulous colour.
You've been over this terrain a thousand times
and suddenly the roadsigns mean nothing
and just as you decide never to return from heaven
you find you've returned, your heart as impossible
to ignore as a flowering horse chestnut tree.

What would the world look like without the eye,
the watery and slightly scum-covered eye, the blossom
opening on the end of a long green stalk
after millennia of blindness? The eye does not
snap open, it opens with the slow emotion
of a brain that has not yet been born, a sacred
organ that knows its existence depends upon
a billion years of devotion to the vague idea of
light, congregations of apes worshipping the moon
and stars all born in the dawn of the eye.

The eye pops open like a pair of lips
and an egg pops out. The pupil is an earnest
pupil and quickly learns the facts of light.
And if you look quickly you will see
new-hatched ospreys fluttering from the
noblest orb. And this is what the thin king
was thinking: the mind is a diamond
the size and shape of the holy grail.

# VIII

Your heart is the source of night's radiance
and music enters your heart like blood,
the heart a perpetual emotion machine
pumping in great relentless troughs and crests
and the view of the stars is blocked by a giant
pine. The Florida manatee weighs a thousand pounds
and its giant heart is continually melting.
And the seagulls of English Bay can astonish you
with the lazy turnings of their awful cries,
the cries the heart would make if it were beaked.
For this is the country of the open heart
where to draw a breath is infinitely strange
and where at times you'll forget that you don't know
who you are and what you're here for
like a long line of monosyllabic footprints
tracking across the beach and into the sea.
But the music will enter your heart like blood
and rainbows will explode inside your clothes!
And the sea will tell you of your lost instincts
and you will enjoy standing on your heart
as the night stands on the knight's heart
and sudden flares illuminate comfortable horizons
which suddenly take to the air and land on the other
side of rows of pyramid-shaped fast-food outlets.
For your most unforgettable dream evolved from a universe
that is rapidly contracting, an intelligence
with a sword in its heart, dying, a universe
in which everything is also a garden
the centre of which is a giant eye that never
closes and a heart that never heals.
And what is most delicious is the loneliness,
most painful the persistent knowledge
that you have not suffered enough,
that you have enjoyed the sweetest realizations
while entire cities have been burnt alive,
schools of dolphins sobbing with uncontrollable
sorrow, and you with your pockets overflowing
with plastic lips, each with a diamond the size
of a tongue-tip at the end of its tongue.

But the night goes on forever, its dark
reptilian attention burning diamond-shaped
patches in the garden of cardinal sin
while intelligent smoke pours into the sky,
and some day you'll return from your sojourn
among the golden isles of mythic romance
and with empty eyes you'll approach your birthplace
and will refuse to tell of what you've seen
and in retaliation your childhood friends
will become like gods again. But you'll be able
to draw a face on the wall and the face
will begin to talk and no one will bother
trying to understand, for you have returned
in the divine night of endless radiance
which surrounds you and is closing in
like new flesh around a bloody wound,
and your mind slithers like smoke through the crack
between an object and its field of space
and a little mercury figure bright as the sun
holds the world aloft from its hollow centre
in brilliant flame, with pride, as if it were
a giant globe weighing but an ounce,
and like two virgins on an elephant's back
night and the brokenhearted universe
experiment with each other's nerve ends
and dream that their flesh is air, water, fire,
and dream of an ancient world aching to be born
along the length of the passionate beach.


## IX

The night is afloat in the mind of the dreamer,
an unusual sort of night, in its way as unusual
as the night of the living dead, and it contains
a billion years of evolutionary light from the stars
and the soft light bathing her features has oozed
out of the pores of her poor skin like mist
swirling in the early morning hills. Her arm
hangs like a falling star. And with each beat
of her heart the earth cools and a spaceship

shoots off into interstellar seas, and somewhere
within that single pulse you see yourself
being born and dying, nothing to be excited about,
and you might see a man dreaming of mermaids
and keeping a Florida manatee in his bathtub,
for radiance gleams on night's imaginary surface
as phosphorescent chemicals glow in the sea
and the night's imaginary surface lies along
the length of the passionate beach of banditry
where your loves and hates are incestuous screens
on which you project your life. Here, in night's
magical radiance where you can dream anything you want
and have anything you want, women everywhere were
laughing themselves to death and men were leaving
meaningless messages for future generations.

The night is afloat in the mind of the dreamer
and the one-eyed light of an approaching train
becomes an illuminating flower from heaven
and the world is a station where such glorious light
shines through occasional chinks to illuminate
the halls of hell. The radiant flower was warm,
with a passion that plunged forth courageously
into further dimensions of *awe* (the sound
the heart makes as it opens a little further).
Every day you age two days
and every night you become one day younger
for time stops when the sun goes down
and the dreamer's life falls apart
for there are too many patterns to smash
and the one pattern she wants can never be found
and the quiet path through the quiet woods
keeps branching and before the branches
reconverge her life will be all but over,
and as soon as one path is chosen it too branches
until she becomes trapped in her own originality,
lost in a grain of sand inexhaustible as a star.
For the mind works better when completely naked,
solemnly flashing in the middle of the night
like a beacon of incredible flesh, a wild blossom
blinking music into deepest space.

And the dreamer is afloat in the radiant night.
Even her phone is off the hook. And the occasional
chinks were tiny windows in the endless halls
of hell where fear and dull convention served
as the cruellest tools of torture eternity
could devise. And the dreamer, mindless, strangely
afloat, drifted up to one of these random cracks
in the character armour of hell, a slot
awash with heaven's intelligent light,
and she placed her blissful eye against the slit
as if it were a voyeur's keyhole or the entrance
to her mother's womb and the world beyond,
and after the sensitive orb adjusted to the light
she sighed and saw in perfect focus and 3-D form
screaming children with their flesh falling off
leaping into the sewers of Hiroshima.

## X

Sunset is a time of consolation, sunrise one
of experience, and between the velvet rays
of night dissolve the mind-carved blocks
that damn the noblest spiritual aspirations
and create a prison for the most light-hearted
dreams, a tomb for youth, bottomless quicksand
for all that is quick. The blocks dissolve
in tremendous foam and mist and the human race
is once again united amid sacrificial feasts
and that which animates one animates all until
the origin of consciousness is finally understood
and everyone sleeps in one another's heart
dreaming they're reliving past lives,
arms and legs entwined like lazy musical theories
unable to differentiate their own identities.
And they are so happy happiness loses its meaning
and evil is a waxed corpse in a glass case
with thousands of angels waiting in sublime lines
to gaze briefly at such embalmed splendour
amid sudden visions of copulating snakes
and images of Miss Universe contests.

Night is a planet blocking its own light
and the furious joy of angels in heat
enters the world like perfumed rain.
Old men on deathbeds finally regret
having spent their lives at war with their senses.
Watermelons left lying in the moonlight
suddenly pop like popcorn.

The night has fourteen rigid principles.
The night is constantly brushing its teeth.
The night is afraid of the dark.

The night blinded Homer on a bet.


## XI

The personality goes down like a raw egg,
like a young kid with new skates who goes out
and scores two goals to win the Stanley Cup.
And there is a certain randomness about infinity
as if you could reach out into the Novalis night
and grab ahold of any kind of magic you desire.
As when you were a child beginning to read
there were mysterious curtains and screens of myth
receding into the brilliance of the past.
As when you were middle-aged, face to face
with indescribable fate, you felt like a
flipped coin poised in the air:
heads your future, tails your past.
As when you were old, the night moving over you
like the blunt instruments of amorous flesh,
and you regretted the patterns of your lies,
lies reflecting a life of dull convention,
a life predicting widespread nuclear warfare
by next Christmas and the Florida manatee
eats a ton of aquatic vegetation every day.

This is the night of endless radiance when all
legends and myths will be placed on instant replay:
Columbus spots a Florida manatee and thinks

he's discovered a mermaid, the *Queen of Nanaimo*
pulls out with three short blasts of its foghorn,
and all is well, it's a pleasant world, as if
you're about to remember where you buried a stash
of diamonds in a previous life and it's all there
waiting for your recovery. For the beautiful dreamer
who used to live across from the Montreal Forum
on hockey nights would watch the crowds going in
and hear the roar when a goal was scored
and that's how she got interested in levitation,
for everyone takes a radio to the Forum
and listens to the game while watching it
and the players become illuminated, naturally,
and play far beyond human knowledge as much
as the intensity of their individual
illumination will allow and there's always
the danger of levitation, players suddenly floating
high above the ice as if it's not harps the angels
play but hockey, and blood spurts out of wounds
in hands and feet and trickles down the face of each
astonished player and sprinkles the crowd like holy
sweat, the crowd becoming hushed, night closing in.
Night closes in and falls into your heart
weary with the burden of being apart.
And the movement of the planets, comets and asteroids
raises and lowers the hair of your flesh
and each star has a billion stories to tell
and the tongue of a poet to tell them with.


## XII


You are examining a leaf on a tree in the vast
northern forests, a grain of lust, a raw oyster
and the sensation as it slithers down a single throat
out of which blossoms a subterranean voice,
yet the throat tries to maintain with its voice
the same kind of intimacy that exists between
a couple through years of careless love
or the kind of identity existing between
a farmer and his fields and the kind

of interfusion existing between cloud and sky.
And the mind expands like a bloating corpse.
The mind reaches out until it touches another mind.
The mind's shape is dictated by the shape of the
minds surrounding it. The mind is touched on all
sides by other minds. The mind is an eye at the
keyhole of all the minds surrounding it. The mind
is a transparent brick, a membrane enclosing hogs
and pyramids and covered with heavenly secretions.

The mind has qualities seldom considered
and can provide comfort in times of stress.
Indeed it possesses the ability to emit
spontaneous waves of sympathy and to predict
general weather patterns. It has an ability
to disappear, a love of appearing and disappearing
here and there, an ability to ejaculate on command,
an ability to attract razor blades, iron filings
and like minds. It has an ability to feel at any
given time what has never been felt before and to suffer
waves of sorrow for dying soldiers in ancient wars.
An ability to entertain the night as a trained bear
entertains the crowd. An ability to train invisible ponies.
An ability to love itself with an absence of passion
more intense than passion itself. An ability to love
itself without thought. An ability to know and remember
nothing but that which is absolutely necessary for survival.
An ability to destroy itself. An ability to destroy
its ability to destroy itself. An ability
to record, erase, play back and fast forward.
An ability to see itself wherever it looks.

The mind has never been mined! At the moment the mind's
love for itself disappears the mind disappears
and mythological creatures come tumbling over the horizon.
Columbus mistakes a Florida manatee for Miss Key West.
A. Y. Jackson sprinkles salt and pepper on a pine forest
north of Lake Inferior. A bouquet of blue irises bursts
into flame. But before it vanishes the mind finds itself
unable to ignore the proliferation of coincidences all the more
touching because of their triviality and persistence.

The hog's ears appeared in the tall grass.
Enormous pyramids appeared across the lake.


## XIII

Night thoughts are bandits unable to resist
the beauty of the naked mind for they find
the mind most beautiful when completely naked.
This diamond the size of the holy grail
reflecting everything all at once
becomes a voluptuous magnet attracting
exotic night thoughts from distant planets
and again these bandits have kidnapped the naked
mind in spite of the great risks involved
for a band of radiation surrounds such nakedness
and as the band of bandits approaches the band
they must devise ways of passing through
without being dissolved instantaneously
into radiant particles of quickly dispersing
static and each new bandit must be more and more
cunning and this is how philosophy is born.

The bandits were weary. They'd travelled from another
hemisphere and were wandering along the passionate
beach, sighing, cursing, wishing they'd never
heard of enchantment. And the waves rolled in
at their feet, wave after wave of natural radiance.
And the bandits sighed again and listened
to the collision of trillions of particles of sand
and the sudden subsiding of the curious crests.
And teams of celestial apes with high-powered
jeeps and rifles roam the countryside:
the apes of wrath, each ape with a diamond
the size and shape of the holy grail
on the end of his neck. And how they love
to kill one another! They hang each other
on ropes and tie each other to stakes
and then set fires. The moans, the screams.
The stars start staring and become startled.
And the pencil casts a long shadow

as civilization disintegrates again and even
saints love to cancel one another out.

But the mind is never naked, the mind
can never be aware of its nakedness
for the concept of a naked mind implies
the stripping of the mind's ability
to know its own nakedness, a condition
of innocence so profound the first thing to go
is the notion of innocence.
And the bandits no longer felt weary.
They looked at each other and saw nothing
but the waves splashing on the grainy sand,
phosphorescent waves in blackest night,
waves insisting on being seen by human eyes
as if their glorious music weren't enough
with its moaning tear-filled climaxes causing
a tremendous shudder to fill the equinox
every ten or fifteen seconds along the length
of the passionate, jam-packed beach.
For it is not the mind that proclaims its own
nakedness and perfect innocence
but rather that which surrounds the mind,
the new romance that moves around it
as water moves around each school of fish,
the waves that splash on the sand-witched beach
and witness the sudden absence of the bandits
for the face that stares out of the mirror
is at least as alive as your own. The innocence
of a bubble that has burst! And the bandits sat down
and sadly listened to Issa's celestial music
and as they listened they simply vanished, ceased
to exist and only the waves and the bewitched sand
seemed to be left. Like the story of Ramakrishna
who saw two boatmen angrily exchanging blows
far out on the Ganges and marks from the blows
immediately appeared on his body, and then
a truck went by and everybody on the street
screamed but Ramakrishna merely smiled
for this was still the nineteenth century
and motor vehicles hadn't even been invented.

Even the driver's blood ran cold
and the bloody hand of a baby fell from the sky.


## XIV

Spring came early this year and produced
incredible dimensions of beautiful banditry
much of it frankly excessive
and produced unusually radiant nights
with the sunset's afterglow hanging in the sky
till the fourth false dawn started telling the truth
and everyone slept thinking all was well,
never dreaming an ugliness terrifying in its banality
was spreading over the world with dozens
of dead and dying dolphins lying along
the length of the compassionate beach. And a ferocious
longing for lost beauty was being attacked in the ring
like a bull while the crowds cried and the bull died
and the spirits of saints hovered in the skies
and a butterfly vomited on John Keats' notebook
and fluttered away like a tiny Pegasus
bearing a wagon heaped with corpses of tiny dreams
and the hog's ears appeared in the tall grass
and a pyramid appeared in one of the ears.
But only two per cent of the civilian population
saw anything, the remainder blinded by their continual
lust for personal glory and an arrogance that will never
melt into the ordinary radiance of the heart.

And people you have never met
but who could have been your dearest friends
are disappearing in the moonless night
while the forest labours to understand
the sound of passing motor vehicles.

And people you have never met
appear crazily in your memories, hungering
for acceptance, ridiculing you for your lost
emotions, the quickly fading images
of a splendid lack of horror —

And someone you have never met
smiles as he stands there reading your mail,
preparing a modest meal with his one free hand —
for the horror is a relic of a radiant mind
and at your heart's core lies the flesh made word
in a tiny pocket of tears where that which can happen
nowhere else can happen, a mathematics of existence
that is heading blindly into outer night
where a world is being transformed again and again.
And at this moment, entering your body,
is a spirit the size of a baseball stadium
as if the sewers of Hiroshima were flooded with dreams,
with stacks of creamcheese sandwiches on small rafts,
and here and there a ladder leading down to a place
where long-lost friends have snowball fights
in summer meadows and peaceful gardens of no desire
where in pools of warm vomit fresh constellations
of human eyes stare up at the starry sky,
and the moon like an ancient bard sings of night
while the stars, lesser medieval rhymesters
sparkling like rare pop bottles from the forties,
whisper magic formulae into the ears of aged
astronomers gazing into their horny helioscopes.

And people you have never met
are living their lives in remote Tibetan villages
waiting for you to pass through and be transformed
by their overwhelming beauty, a beauty
only you can see, so that your life becomes
bent like light passing through a black star,
a warp that will ache and ache forever
and you can watch movies every day
and scan crowd scenes in slow motion
and you will never find yourself
or anyone else you could possibly be
for you are trapped in the trap you set for others
like someone trying to swim Lake Ontario
with Lakes Erie and Huron strapped to his back, poetry
a process for stabbing the heart with heart-felt lines
of icy darkness, poetry the art of darkness,
and tiny people swim for the furthest shore

in the red glow of a Canadian sunset,
each frantic swimmer and entire universe
hoping not to die and laughing playfully
as his or her lungs fill with real blood
along the length of passion's peach-strewn beach.

And on this spot three thousand years ago stood a
beautiful naked boy, a string of fish in each hand.

# Country Hotel in the Niagara Peninsula

The guy was shooting pool. I stopped to watch.
He missed an easy shot and the cue ball
hopped the cushion and crashed to the floor.
"I'm bad luck," I murmured apologetically
as I scurried to the door. "You sure are,"
the guy yelled after me, his voice melting
into the evening fog, streaked with light from the
streetlamps and the headlights of cars on Highway 8.

Everybody understands my poetry. There is nothing
hidden. A large mind examines a small mind,
mounts it like a butterfly, splits it open
under intense light, an ongoing autopsy
in the morgue of all our lives.
You know everything you need to know.

# Anticipating a Trip to Ontario

Wearing a watch that once belonged
to Robert Louis Stevenson
the famous actor David Niven
sat at the kitchen table questioning my wisdom
in having pictures of you on the wall.
We'd been eating cream cheese and tomato sandwiches.
A full moon was setting behind the Kokanee Glacier
like a blob of butter dissolving in hot tea.
Suddenly he coughed and slumped in his chair
and his wife said my God he's had a heart attack,
and then he vanished in a puff of invisible smoke.
I looked all around the room, even under the table.
Eerie pounding noises started coming from the walls.
I looked at the cream cheese on the table.
The expiry date was on the wrapper: June 7.
By then, I thought, I'll be in Ontario.

# Dying Metaphors
*—after George Orwell's "Politics and the English Language"*

RING THE CHANGES ON.

Little Abbie Hands stood on top of Terry Fox Mountain, took the ring off her finger and flung it over the side, then sighed. The binoculars were the next to go and then her clothing, her little children, the dog, the family car, the sort of thing your left hand might write all on its own as you sit reading Iris Murdoch novels, your heart stuffed with family photos, and somebody is staring at you through the window and you hope it's somebody you haven't seen since grade 6.

A man who vows to give his voice to the dreams of others.

TAKE UP THE CUDGELS FOR.

Cudgels are stout sticks used for beating the brains out of bad guys. What is that smell? The smell of new brains being born, a train of newborn babies steaming down the Sante Fe trail at midnight with a full moon and neat rows of palmettos.

You could take one of these sticks and break all the hearts on your block. Love is like milk, you have to keep it on ice. Shakespeare: They that love best their loves shall not enjoy.

TOE THE LINE.

David, what are you doing? I cannot tell a lie. I am towing a lion from here to Cour d'Alene. And did you know there are more lions in Idaho than Ontario?

David, I want your heart to be open for love at all times.

My name is Toe. I'm a line. You can call me a contemporary non-metrical form. David is such a lovely lion-thrower but where does he get his lions from and how does he know when to quit?

You always quit when you least want to.

RIDE ROUGHSHOD OVER.

David, why don't you hop on your bike and ride over to Roughshod right away? Your mother always used to say here's a quarter, run over to the store and get me eleven cents' worth of monkey mucus and a nickel's worth of sandwich sperm — and make sure the sperm is slimy. Then I'll make you the loveliest lunch.

David's mother gets angry when we call him David. So when she's around we call him Shitface. And she's going to be around until November. David's problem is he's overly roughshod. Most people around here wear ballet slippers if anything.

STAND SHOULDER TO SHOULDER WITH.

It's too late. If you really wanted to come you would have been here by now. Suddenly his face changed colour. I had a hunch he was about to hunch his shoulders, even though I knew it was almost lunchtime. When he hunched them I said I knew you were going to do that and he merely shrugged his shoulders with typical Gallic charm.

The sandblasters knew all about standing shoulder to shoulder and all that that entails. Two thats in a row. That's that.

PLAY INTO THE HANDS OF.

I was walking around all day down by the river with my hands cut off at midstream. I was feeling sad inside. When all at once they nabbed me for playing left wing and lopped off my lovely paws.

Don't listen to him. He just wants you to play into his hands. But he doesn't have hands. Not today maybe but you see him tomorrow and he'll have hands aplenty to torment you with.

Dear Abbie Hands, how I love to torment you. My hands these days are full of amorous purpose. One of my hands played into the other. Which reminds me: what have you done with my Swiss army knife?

NO AXE TO GRIND.

Suddenly I found myself facing the emptiness of a blank piece of paper and remembering what I was born for. And so I started writing and ideas flew onto the page like little black cigars.

This is the great emptiness Bodhidharma spoke of, the great well of peace alluded to by all the holy women of the past.

We have no axe to grind. Who cares if Abbie Hands is sleeping with Tom in Philadelphia tonight (gasp!)? Grind coffee, not axes.

GRIST TO THE MILL.

You never know when you're going to upset the gods. You could be just floating along for forty years and suddenly these words appear: Grist to the mill. Two spectators were killed and six injured at the start of the Ninth Balsam River Marathon and Second World River Boat Championships.

Oh David, come home. I want you back with me forever. I want to play dying metaphors into your hands. This is your old friend Abbie Hands speaking, smoking little black cigars and writing down by the old mill stream.

FISHING IN TROUBLED WATERS.

Don't you love the twenties? The styles, the flames licking up our spines. We were sailing along on Moonlight Bay when we heard the white folks singing these words: Fishing in troubled waters.

Boy, was I scared. There were people getting lynched all around me. Once I realized how troubled I'd been I couldn't get enough fishing in.

## The Night Watchman

In the finest writing there's a magic
that will outlive marble and the fame of tyrants,
and in the most ordinary writing, if honest,
there's a seed of magic that grows and grows
                              and blossoms with time,
and you've been dead thirty years,

and today I read some of your writings,
unpublished works never intended to be published
in fact it would be criminal to publish them,

and I read them aloud to a friend
and we crassly speculated on your motives
in recording the things you recorded:
the daily weather, the results
of bouts between boxers long dead,
the births and deaths of neighbours,
the dates of battles that now seem insignificant
and the receiving and sending of letters
now forgotten.

I said you probably knew the act of writing
was magic, and moved you automatically
into deeper, more refreshing streams.

My friend, less charitable, thought you recorded
to record, to settle arguments, to structure
memory, fashioning a weapon to prove
the most contentious points.
                              And I suppose
we were both aware we were speculating on love
and other inevitable natural forces
and there were no answers

for there was a holiness in your writing
that was meant for you alone
and our jaded eyes were like the direct rays

of the noonday sun on tender seedlings

and again I hold your books, to me
more precious than the rarest tomes
and deep within me I feel our worlds touch
like the sensitive roots of adjacent trees.

# How I'd Like to Die

I'd like to be swallowed alive by a giant anaconda
and the poor thing would have to lug me around inside it
until there was nothing left of me
but a small pearl of wisdom.

I'd like to whip out a knife and stab myself to death
while delivering a sentimental speech at a family reunion,
the knife a magic one handed down generation by generation
from neolithic times and to be used only
for circumcision and severing the umbilical cord.

I'd like to drown while frolicking with nuns
in a private swimming pool
filled with warm tapioca pudding.

I'd like to be sitting in the lotus posture
in the centre of a totally dark and silent room
until everything became so still
there'd be no need to draw another breath
and I'd have to be buried in a pyramid-shaped box
with a pleasant look on my face
and no signs of rot having set in.

I'd like to starve to death
while managing a busy and successful delicatessen.

I'd like to be hanged
for attempting to assassinate Hitler.

I'd like to be machine-gunned while trapped in barbed wire
at Dieppe, seasick, drenched, in 1942,
along with all the other guys
from the Royal Hamilton Light Infantry.

I'd like to die laughing in the front row of the Bloor Cinema
during the rabbit-hunting scene in *Rules of the Game*
with my friend Christopher at my side, embarrassed,

pretending he didn't know me.

I'd like to meet, by chance, my mystical twin soul,
someone to whom I'd be so attracted and who
would be so attracted to me
that our hearts would stop
and our souls would lift off into angelic realms.

I would not like to die in a nuclear holocaust.

# Return of the Native

I was sad to be leaving the west and had a strange
feeling I'd never see you or British Columbia again
and wished we'd spent more time walking in the mountains,
sleeping under the stars, watching Canadian sunsets, but
perennial wisdom says the universe out there and the universe
in here is the same old universe.

I drove east through the interior of British Columbia
through winding mountain roads all through the night
and the deer and elk came down and stood at the roadside
as if to watch the car go by,
as if to say goodbye, Dave,
we're going to miss you but we understand you have to go

and a couple of days later I was driving
down through the rolling hills north of Lake Superior
at dawn, red sun shining through mist as thick as whipped cream,
and the mist lifted for a moment and I saw something standing
in the road a mile ahead so I cut my engine and coasted
and it was a moose, full-grown, female, tall and elegant,
and it stood there watching as I coasted up to it
and it seemed to be saying
welcome home, Dave, we missed you, and not until
I came to a full stop a foot from its nose did it turn
and run off into the forest.

# Malcolm Lowry

Been dead twenty-two years and still you come around a tear-filled Vancouver street and there you are face to face with his spirit, the old Caroline Apartments on Nelson Street, its canopy tattered and torn, the bricks darker, everything darker. And that must be the YMCA, he used to complain about the noise when it was being built, and now look how old it looks.

What a gamble to let feelings become deep! It doesn't matter what you feel as long as you feel, and to be a writer and have to record the details of this ultimate gamble, a small ship on a stormy sea, to value, as he put it, dread above all human feelings.

He gambled so much and his greatness was human, spiritual, non-literary. Even if you are a man you want to take this man to your breast but you know eternity itself couldn't console him and he was the *Verbum Dei,* I think, come to earth to tell us there is no consolation, there is nothing but the individual human being.

# Pinnochio

It seems strange now but when you and I were first married
and I was going to medical school
I used to bring home small cadavers
to work on over the weekend.
I can remember walking down the street
holding a dead baby
unwrapped
as if it were a doll.
I must have been rather thoughtless in those days.
The neighbours must have thought I was practising
up to be a ventriloquist.

One night I was bringing home the body
of an infant with an unnaturally large nose.
Such a long thin nose
would have looked strange even on an adult.
For a joke I dressed the dead kid
up in a pair of lederhosen
and the kind of blouse and cap
you tend to associate with Pinnochio.
As I walked along under the streetlamps
I heard kids whispering
hey look
he's got Pinnochio!

But you weren't one for such jokes.
It was about ten-thirty and I was hoping
you'd be upstairs reading
but you were in the kitchen drinking tea
and I knew you'd be upset
if I walked in with the baby
dressed up like that
so I tossed it under the porch.
I figured I'd wait
until you were asleep
and then retrieve it.

But when I went back out a few hours later
it was gone.
I never did find out what happened to it.
Maybe raccoons dragged it off.
Maybe it came back to life
like Pinnochio
and ran away.

# Greaseball

You glance at the motorcyclist who's just passed you
driving north out of Nanaimo
and you notice his right leg is horribly misshapen
and his pant leg is rolled up to his thigh
exposing a horrible scar
that twists around the upper leg
like the annulus of a mushroom
and his lower leg is shorter than it should be
and extends outwards strangely
for there is no knee with which to bend it
and there are only three toes on the foot.

You figure he's injured his leg in an accident
and is quite brave to be riding again
for it looks as if he's lost his leg
and had another grafted on
although that's crazy
but soon he is lost to sight
and you think no more of him.

Until you stop at a gas station
and while your tank is being filled
you go into the garage to price tires
and there is the same motorcyclist
washing the floor with a mop
and along with him
is a younger man
and the younger man
has a similarly misshapen leg
and his pant leg is similarly rolled up
showing an identical scar
the same missing knee
the same three toes.

And the younger guy has a dog
and when you nervously go to pat the dog
the dog growls.

Easy now, Greaseball,
calls out the younger fellow
as he opens a package of liver
and tosses it on the floor
and the dog jumps at it
and starts eating it

and there is the most beautiful smell
of lilacs in the air.

# Thirty-four Lines about Horses

If you slice open the brain of a dead horse you'll often find
tiny hooves imbedded in the centre of each lobe.
From the tops of hills horses can see the sea.
When a horse first senses the approach of spring
he will place his lips three inches from the left ear
of another horse and stand like that all afternoon.
Horses stare at the road and never move their heads
even when trucks full of horses roar by.
It's bad luck to argue about horses.
There is a herd of wild horses on the moon.
When a horse is shot horses all over the world tremble.
A horse in Blind River, Ontario, has a small bank account.
There are no horses in British Columbia.
A lie about a horse is not a real lie.
Horses love cigar smoke.
A horse knows when you have bet on him.
In 1949, a pilot, having had an argument with his fiancée,
pushed her horse out of a plane flying over Toronto at
       3,000 feet.
LSD has no effect on horses.
Horses love the smell of telephones.
Horses love to carry beautiful naked women on their bare backs.
Horses love to have their eyes kissed by nuns.
Horses dream they are horses.
The average horse wants to be famous some day.
Horses love people with bad breath.
Horses are proud of their beautiful bodies.
A horse will develop high blood pressure if you cut off its tail.
Horses like to fantasize about making love to whales.
Horses love to eavesdrop on human conversation.
Horses barely tolerate the chirping of birds.
A horse will go out of its way to avoid a Seventh Day Adventist.
Horses are particularly fond of pregnant women.
When a horse is shown pictures of beautiful mountains
its brain begins to produce theta waves.
Horses love to be visited by horses from other countries.
Horses hate it when you run your fingernails down the blackboard.

# The Bunny Farm

There was a crabapple tree with small green apples lying on the grass like short-stemmed mushrooms. Someone picked up one of the apples and threw it over the fence into the bunny farm. Most of the bunnies didn't notice it but maybe seven of them did. Seven came running towards the spot where the apple landed but before they got there most of them forgot what they were running for and veered off into other directions. One rabbit, perhaps of superior intelligence, did not forget what he was running for and made it right to the apple. He took a little nip out of it then went away. One of the other rabbits who had been running towards the apple but made a wrong turn accidentally came upon the apple a little while later. He sniffed at it then he too took a nip out of it then went away. All this time the big black rabbit, the one that appeared to be the boss rabbit of the bunny farm, was lying on top of a newcomer, pumping furiously with his hindquarters. The newcomer was a small, distracted-looking rabbit with white tips at the ends of its ears.

It was beginning to get dark and a full moon was rising over Lake Ontario. There was an observation tower in the middle of the farm complex, with floodlights. The floodlights came on. All night long there would be someone in that tower watching the animals, making sure no harm came to them. One time a man jumped over the fence and started making love to the female donkeys. He said the beautiful women on the beach had got him all worked up. Another time someone stole three goats. One was recovered. It had been found running wild in a high-rise apartment building in Mount Hope. The other two had been eaten. The guy who was on duty in the tower lost his job over that one. It turned out he was a friend of the guy who stole the goats. Every day billions of things happen and are forgotten.

But I meant to talk only about the bunny farm, not the goat farm and the donkey farm. At least I managed to avoid talking about the cows, ducks, pheasants, peacocks, chickens and roosters. The roosters, two of them, are in the same enclosure as the rabbits. If a rabbit gets too close the roosters peck out his eyes with their beaks. That's life.

Sometimes a rabbit will jump up into the air for no reason at all. People stand at the fence watching the bunnies and envy their idyllic existence. When one of the bunnies starts running around seemingly for no reason at all sometimes a little kid will say look at that, Speedy Gonzales. Sometimes one of the small bunnies, maybe only five inches from nose to tail, will be running and fall into a hole. It's fun to watch them pull themselves out of the holes which are really quite shallow of course.

Sometimes during the night a mushroom will grow right in the middle of the bunny farm. In the morning a bunny will find it and eat it. Let's hope it's not a poisonous mushroom. It's no fun being sick even when you're a rabbit.

And oh yes in the bunny farm is a beautifully designed set of wooden shelters where the rabbits can go to keep dry when it rains. But this is just to satisfy people who complain that there's no place for the rabbits to go when it rains. Because the rabbits never go in there, not even when it's raining really hard. They just stay out and get wet.

# The Cow That Swam Lake Ontario

A curious story is mine to tell
and I must tell thee of it.
It is serious and much more curious
than that multitude of stories —
so frequent they have come to bore us —
of household pets, dogs and cats,
who have been taken from their homes
and placed in new homes far from their old
and somehow by what stars we know not
have hastened back to their ancient domiciles.
Such stories by their very frequency
have lost their ability to enthrall us, to remind us
of the unfathomable mysteries of existence.
And this story is even more curious
than those less frequent stories
such as the one concerning the dog of Flanders
belonging to a man who left it with his family
when he was temporarily assigned to a new post
in a distant land. The dog vanished
from his home and weeks later discovered
his master in a land in which it had never been before.
This story, my friends, concerns a cow,
a member of a lowly race
considered unable to partake of divine grace,
a race of ignorant, dim-witted beasts
who amuse us only by their ability
to fill our palates with intense pleasure
and our stomachs with bovine bliss.
We have marked, of course, how cows
tend to become somewhat rebellious
while being led to slaughter
but this does not necessarily indicate
an ability to foretell their bloody fate
by any wondrous sense of pre*cow*gnition
but merely indicates the cow hath an ear
with which to hear the loathsome cries of fear
of its sisters who have gone before.

And we know that on occasion
a cow will try to leap the barricades
and sometimes be successful.
These are perhaps worthier specimens
with the insane urge to survive
more strongly etched in their genetic code —
the nobles of cattledom you might say —
but almost invariably they are surrounded
by men with ropes and guns
and seldom make it far away
from their fateful road to Calvary.
For unlike dogs and cats, the cow
finds it difficult to blend with its locale,
finds it difficult to move unnoticed
in areas where it is not usually found.
A cow wandering along a city street
would immediately arouse suspicion
and you seldom see signs in stores
saying no cows allowed. . . .

Anyway, on the evening of October 11 —
I remember it well for it was my birthday —
I was in a borrowed motorboat fishing for salmon
on Lake Ontario just beyond the Burlington canal
through which giant Great Lakes steamers
in fact huge ships from all around the world
enter the factory-lined waters of Hamilton Harbour
when I heard what I thought was a salmon
skipping along on the surface as they often do
and turning I was surprised to see
a bovine head, with two shining horns
and two eyes as full and calm as fresh-plucked plums,
ploughing steadfastly through the starry waves
heading, and for this I checked my map and compass,
in the direction of Prince Edward County
that peninsula on the north shore
two hundred kilometres across the cold night waters
of lovely Lake Ontario.

Of course I pulled my line and quietly followed
at a respectful distance, knowing the very presence

of an observer frequently alters that which is observed,
and I was surprised to find what must seem absurd —
the beast was proceeding in a line so straight
and at such a steady pace, without diverging
one degree in either direction from its course,
it made me think a seasoned sea captain
could take lessons from this lowly animal.
It was proceeding at maybe half a knot
as a full moon spilled a splash of light
and sparkled off its horns
and I lagged behind with my motor idling
at a speed suitable for trolling for salmon
until I was at a point where the bovine head
was about to disappear into the distance
and I kept at that distance
all through the night
following that awesomely purposeful beast
as it ploughed through the black and golden waves
straighter than the deadliest arrow
and as I putted along back a quarter of a mile
I sipped coffee and for a while
imagined I was the coach of Marilyn Bell.
And by the time the rosy fingers of the sun
took over from the slowly setting moon
the task of illuminating this strange scene
I began to feel a sense of senseless love
towards the cow I was so senselessly following
for I was not following it with the hope
of somehow capturing it and slaughtering it
and taking its carcass home for my freezer
but rather I was following it
out of the deepest curiosity
and a kind of non-anthropomorphic devotion
for I didn't even know that cows could swim
never mind swim the width of Lake Ontario.

The dawn was quiet as the night had been.
The sound of the softly turning motor of my boat
and the watery whisper of the swimming beast
had calmed my mind to a silence so profound
I could hear the slow soft thumping of my heart.

And slowly as we continued across the lake
in a line so straight I thought my heart would break
the dawn turned into brilliant day
and beyond the black hypnotic head of this fearless beast
a thin blue line rose above the horizon
and I checked my map and compass once again
and realized we were approaching
the shore of Prince Edward County.

We passed Wicked Point and the lighthouse of Point Petre
and entered a lovely bay known as Soup Harbour
which was named so the story goes
after a ship loaded with kegs of powdered soup
was wrecked in a storm a hundred years ago,
a ship so large and so filled with soup
the wives of settlers in the area
for weeks after carried pails of water
home from the bay and boiled the water down
and served delicious soup for supper.

The sun was almost at its zenith
and from my vantage point half a mile out
I watched as the cow's hooves struck shallow bottom
and it raised its weary body and stumbled ashore
and fell exhausted on the warm dry sand.
But it didn't rest long. It soon arose,
staggered up across a narrow gravel bar,
its udder blue and puckered, barely swinging,
and slipped into a grove of maple trees.

It seemed strange there was no one on the shore
to greet us, no television cameras,
no hordes of well-wishers, no local politicians,
no corporate executives to shower my nameless friend
with free cars and other expensive gifts
for after all her feat was just as great
as those of Marilyn Bell and other mighty swimmers
who have conquered as they say the cold black waters
of lovely Lake Ontario.
But I didn't dwell on what might have been.
I pulled the boat up on the shore

and ran towards the grove of trees
anxious not to let the cow out of my sight
for after following her quietly through the night
I certainly deserved at the very least
to discover the destination of this beast,
to discover the reason behind her odyssey,
and if I lost her now I'd spend my life
torturing myself for having let her go.

Once I reached the trees I stopped and listened
and heard in the distance the crunching sound
of heavy hooves on the forest floor
and followed the sound until I came to a clearing
and there I saw a sight so endearing
I'll remember it as long as I live
and maybe even longer.

Just beyond the clearing was a pasture
enclosed by a well-built barbed-wire fence
and in the pasture a good-sized herd of cows
and as you might have guessed some bulls as well
lazily grazed on green grass in the sun.
And there was the cow I'd followed through the night —
my cow as I'd come to think of her —
standing outside the fence looking in.
And as I watched a large black bull looked up,
saw her, and broke into a run.
And several cows and calves came also over
as if welcoming my cow home after a holiday.
And after sniffing each other's noses for a while
the bull, the cows and calves backed up a bit
and my cow crouched down as if about to sit,
then with one mighty leap leaped over the fence.

The nearest town to there was Cherry Valley,
about four miles away. I tried to thumb
but no one would pick me up. I guess
after such a night I looked a mess.
So I walked to town and ate a meal
then phoned home and arranged

to have a car and trailer
driven around the lake
to pick up my borrowed motorboat.
And then I made a few long-distance calls
to various meatplants and slaughterhouses
in the area around Hamilton and Burlington
and after a few calls I talked to a guy
who said they'd had a nice shipment the day before
of cattle from a farm way up on the north shore
and from that shipment one cow had jumped
from the ramp leading to the abattoir
and got away before they could recapture her
but they were planning to start looking for her again
in the woods around Cootes Paradise,
a little bay that flows into Hamilton Harbour.
You'll never find her there, I said,
and then hung up.

And so I went home and wrote this poem
without even bothering to wash my hands
or change my clothes. And now
I'm coming to the end of it
and as you can imagine I'm really tired,
although not as tired as that cow must have been
after its great escape from the camp of death.
And I know whoever reads this won't believe me
they'll think it's just a lot of bull
and not even very well written.

All I can say is this:
following that cow across that lake
was the most poetic experience of my life
and I just had to write a poem about it.
And maybe that great escape and marathon swim
gave the brave cow only a couple of days more life.
Maybe she went back to the meat plant in the next shipment.
And maybe this time she wasn't able to escape.
Beef cattle are on the same level of anonymity
as earthworms, minnows, and the untold thousands
who built the Pyramids of Egypt. The farmer

never would have noticed her return.
And her eventual fate I'll probably never learn.
But maybe, my friends, at some future date
I'll find her lying on my supper plate.

# 1982

It snowed all night and in the morning
I went out in my boots and tramped these words
ten feet high in the field above my house:
*These are the snows of yesteryear.*

Birds watched from the boughs of trees
and shivered. I took photos.

In the spring when I had the film developed
the pictures didn't turn out. I did this
for you, poetry lovers. I tried. Failure
isn't as good as success but it's better
than nothing. Next winter, when it snows again,
I will have forgotten this, and even if I haven't,
I'll be too busy for such frivolity. Or maybe
I'll be dead, or, if it matters, permanently
in residence in Tahiti (much the same thing).

# Little Bird in the Mountains

The Greyhound driver had a sleeve-badge
reading SAFETY 27 YEARS
and I said, "Is that consecutive?"
and he just laughed and continued laughing
as he drove that bus flat out in the pre-dawn light
a crescent moon and Venus hanging over Osoyoos
and straight up via a series of hairpin switchbacks
straight up from the floor of the Okanagan Valley
to the top of Anarchist Mountain
the road packed with hard snow
and we met the dawn there at the summit, the sun
splashing merrily in our faces,
and there at the side of the road, at the edge
of a cliff dropping straight down a thousand feet
fluttered a little flock of chickadees
and just then we hit one of them
with the sound of a small clenched fist
breaking.

# The Concept of Egolessness

Remember when you were talking to the Rinpoche
and voicing your concerns about my writing?
Last night on the phone you were talking about
the weekend you drove the Rinpoche to Lake Louise
and he told you he felt he and I were much alike.
He said, remembering his previous talk with you I guess,
that I could write beautiful poetry but chose not to
and he said he was like that, he could be a perfect lama
but chose to be outrageous

                        and when you said that
I just smiled in the dark and could see the Rinpoche
smiling. And yesterday you asked me
what I'd been doing to my hair. And you laughed
when I said I'd got sick of it sticking up all over
and brushed it more than usual that morning.
When I got to a mirror I saw why you'd laughed.
It was sticking up twice as much as usual.

# New York

Frank O'Hara used to say he couldn't enjoy a
blade of grass unless there was a subway handy;
he spent a month in Boston and when he returned
complained about how provincial they were up there.
This year five people already have been killed
by pieces of masonry falling from tall buildings
and eleven people have been killed by demonic comics
who sneak up behind people in subway stations
when the moon is full and push them in front of trains
but there is no fear in New York for I am here
walking with friends down Fifth Avenue on Easter Sunday.
There is a De Chirico exhibit at the Museum of Modern Art
but it is so warm and sunny outside and the streets are so full
of happy people gawking at the fire eaters and the trumpet trios
in front of St. Patrick's Cathedral, and here is a religious
argument, an old guy with bad teeth is holding a Bible
and yelling at this young ordinary-looking guy
and telling him to wipe that smile off his face
because the Bible is serious business
and the young guy says Christ put that smile on my face
and I'm not taking it off, and the old guy tells the young guy
he's a coward, too cowardly to get down on his knees and pray,
and the young guy is a little embarrassed, a crowd is forming,
and I yell out yeah, get down, get down, and the young guy
gets down on his knees with a sigh and he and the old guy pray
and Valerie and I walk on, we seem to have lost Sarah and Kenny
and Jim but we know they'll show up.

                                         In an Indian restaurant
I overhear a man saying to a woman I know what you're going
       to say
and I agree with you, and I think God that could have been me.
And I overhear a stockbroker ask his friend
is that Copper Lake any good? And as Frank O'Hara
lay on his death bed
in Bayview General Hospital
in Mastic Beach

dying of abdominal injuries
after being hit by the left fender of a dune buggy at Fire Island
he joked with the nurse who was French
and insisted on speaking French with her
and Valerie bought a canvas bag marked MoMA
at the Museum of Modern Art where O'Hara used to work
and now I am heading west into British Columbia
where everything is beautiful
and the air is pure
and the water is pure
and there is a general lack of urban blight
and in a moment I will board the plane for Vancouver
and there will be a small delicate sophisticated woman in her
     thirties
sitting next to me and reading French newspapers
and she will order Tia Marias and milk
and I will order bloody Marys
and we will taste each other's breakfasts
and we will talk about Bonnard and Matisse
and I will tell her about Frank O'Hara
and she will tell me about Mayakovsky
how he was always striking up wonderful conversations
with strange and beautiful women in public places
and we will confess to each other
that we are primarily interested
in the quiet life.

# Canada / My Earliest Memory
JULY 1944

Saturday. The big kids on the block
took me to the Avalon on Ottawa Street.
I can't remember the name of the movie
but it was a romantic comedy, had nothing
to do with the war. Halfway through
Margaret went to the john and Alex said
that's Margaret up on the screen you know
and I said no it's not, Margaret's a brunette
and that girl's blonde and he said they dyed
her hair, she just went backstage and became
part of the movie. I thought about it.
Forty years later I'm still thinking about it.
Still wishing I could go backstage,
become part of the movie.

On the way home the big kids
pulled me on my wagon, poet
as parasite. Poet, get a job,
and there was a plane flying low
northwest over the east end of Hamilton
and it was dragging a large bomb-like
canister (they were spraying for mosquitoes)
and I said what's that plane?
That's a German plane, said Alex,
they're going to drop that big huge bomb
on your grandmother's house.
And I believed him. My grandmother
lived off Beach Road near the steel works
and all her sons were in the war
and grandpa had just died. I began crying,
put my head down on the slats of the wagon
and cried and Alex kept pulling.
When I stopped crying I began noticing
through the spaces between the slats of the wagon
the sidewalk cracks passing by.

This was at the corner of Cannon and Balmoral
across from Herb Shorer's Cities Service.
The Avalon is now called the Avon.

# Truckers at a Truckstop

Talking softly about the insignificance
of our lives, and in their voices
traces of an unimaginable awe.
"I'm no one's slave," one of them says.

They have death in their eyes, the light
they reflect is the light of death, the eyes
move as if they've been long dead, and you too
are merely a visual echo of something that never existed.

Death could come so quickly. Braking too hard
to avoid a family stopping in the fast lane to gawk
and even as you brake you know that's it, goodbye mom,
and over and over you go, and it's not so unpleasant.

And the walls of the truck cave in on your flesh
like hitting a can of tuna with a hammer.

So you dress like a cowboy because that's the way
you want to dress, it makes you feel good,
and you haul loads of fruit and machinery
and don't give a damn about your fat belly.

# The Seduction of Queen Elizabeth II

What a day this has been! I don't have any legs and I just finished seducing Queen Elizabeth II! It was about four months ago that I first decided to seduce the Queen. Some jealous fanatic heard about my plans and shot off my legs. I'm still not recovered but when I woke up this morning I just knew today was the day. I dreamt I was being chased by an army of ants. When I looked close each ant was goosestepping and had a little Hitler moustache. Just like the old philosopher in the death camp I dived into the latrine — the one place they wouldn't follow me.

I woke up and noted the pain in my stumps had decreased. It usually does after I dream about ants. So I knew this was the day. For practice I went over to my parents' place and seduced my mom and dad. I sent my dad to the store for some beer and while he was gone I seduced my mom. Then when my mom was in the garden picking me a bouquet of forget-me-nots I seduced my dad. Boy, did he love it! Then I went home and sent my wife over to the welfare office to see about my new motorized wheelchair. While she was gone I seduced my children, all of them, two boys and two girls ages nine to fifteen. Boy, were they surprised!

Then I nipped over to Buckingham Palace and seduced the Queen. It was really quite easy. I wheeled in backwards so it looked as if I were coming out. I wheeled right up to the Queen's rooms and there she was counting her money. I told her I knew something that was even more fun than counting your money. "Oh?" she said, her nostrils all aquiver. "And what would that be, pray tell?" Next thing she knew we were in the royal sack. Maybe I don't have any legs but I could still stand at attention. Imagine me, David McFadden, in bed with the Queen! It didn't last long though for after a few minutes my stumps started to hurt and I had to withdraw. She was obviously terribly disappointed to see me go but, as befits a Queen, she didn't ask when she could see me again. Not sure I'd want to anyway, I mean some things you really only need to do once, right?

And how would I rate the Queen in bed? Superior. Best I've had in fact. Worth losing your legs over? That's a tough question. It's true I'll never walk again like an ordinary person. And yet I'll always have the memory of having had the best in bed.

# Velma's Giant Cinnamon Buns

Some day I'll permanently run out of passion. My idea
of fun will be tapioca pudding for dessert
or maybe on special occasions rhubarb and custard
which my mother used to make when I was a child.
I was the champion eater of raw rhubarb, the envy
of the other kids on the block, but secretly
preferred it cooked, sitting under a layer
of yellow custard with a cherry in the middle.

Let's say I'm eighty and dying.
I won't give a damn. Life, death,
what difference will it make? Right now
I feel richer than Picasso because I know you (and he didn't)
but when I'm eighty and I find out that you've just died
even that won't bother me. We're all just molecules.
Dangerous talk but true.

This is what I wrote on a notebook propped
against my steering wheel driving east across Saskatchewan
on Canada Day. Why is a hangman like a journalist?
They both have a nose for noose. The current
is the only thing swift about Swift Current.

The root of everything is rot.

And as penance for having written this I stopped
at a roadside restaurant with a sign saying
VELMA'S GIANT CINNAMON BUNS
and ordered one. It was sickening,
floating in a pool of butter, and Velma
stood over me, making sure I ate every soggy crumb.

On one side of the highway was the Paradise Motel (SORRY)
and on the other side the Alberta Motel (VACANCY).

I tried to be nice, I said I bet you have the biggest

cinnamon buns in all of Alberta. She wasn't pleased.
This is Saskatchewan, she said.

And they say I have no social conscience!

# Natural History of Cages

He couldn't stand being near the baby, stopped
talking, started staying out all night, then moved
to another coast, took up another life,
lost touch, probably married another wife—

We're just like animals, I said, and Christopher's
eyes flashed, knowing people, even the gentlest,
even the most enlightened, are, I'm sure, full of the
wildest and most wondrous obedience to nature.

And the cub in the Buffalo Zoo playfully nipped
a touch too hard on the tail of the father lion
and the lion batted the cub across the cage, enraging
the lioness who pounced on her mate and bit off his ear.

Years after I witnessed this little event I began having
nightmares of being a lion trapped in a deep dark pit.

## After Reading Shiki's Poem about the Dead Dog Floating down the River

Why do humans live so long?
The dogs I knew in my childhood
are all dead
the cats
the birds
and even that big black horse I used to ride
on my Uncle Cecil and Aunt Clara's farm
is dead, and the farm is now a subdivision
and Uncle Cecil and Aunt Clara are divorced
but they're still alive

and the children I played with
are living quiet lives here and there
and I imagine them
fat
unhappy

and while I'm asking childish questions
how did I manage to be born in the
twentieth century
and why did I used to wake up at night
afraid to die
and hating everybody?

What happened to all that poison
that was building up inside me?

It's two-thirty in the morning
and on the street below
a man is trying to break open
the newspaper vending box
to steal the quarters
and whenever a cruiser goes by
he stops bouncing the box up and down
and pretends to be buying a paper

and then there's Shiki
dying at thirty-five
his stomach bloated with persimmons
sad because he knew
he would never read or write another poem.

# Secrets of the Universe

You're waiting for a bus at Ward and Baker
and a woman comes up to you
and asks for a dance.

You tell her you don't want to dance
for there is too much snow
and not enough music
and she says you didn't mind
dancing with me last night.

And when you tell her she's mistaken
you didn't dance with her or anyone last night
she says oh yes you did
and when you ask where
she says up there
on the roof
and she points to the roof of Hipperson Hardware.

In fact, she says, as her voice drops
and a shy look comes into her eyes
I've even danced with you on other planets
Venus and Mars for example
and then she walks away

leaving you to wonder about the part of your life
that is secret even from you.

# Margaret Hollingsworth's Typewriter

I was eating scrambled eggs in the Shamrock Restaurant
and the eggs tasted like Chinese food
so I said to the waitress I'm a person
who likes Chinese food but doesn't like
my eggs in the morning to taste like chicken fried rice
and she laughed and said it must have been
the green onions and suggested the next time
I come into the Shamrock for breakfast
I specify that I want Canadian green onions
with my scrambled eggs or I'll get Chinese again

and I said there won't be another time,
this is it, I'm a widely respected Canadian writer and editor
and well-regarded in the community too
and shouldn't have to subject myself
to such bad food. I'm finished, I said.
This used to be my favourite Irish-Chinese restaurant
in the entire West Kootenay
but this is it, I'm never coming back —
and through the kitchen door I could see
the Chinese chef covering his ears with his hands.

And so I went to pay my bill
and this is the really embarrassing part,
this is why I'm writing this poem
by hand, pencil on paper, because Margaret Hollingsworth's
typewriter has a three-prong plug
and all the outlets in the house are two-prongers
and her adapter is up at the college
and I begged her to let me cut the third prong off
so I could use her typewriter
because I had a simply overwhelming
desire to write this poem and she refused
and I told . . . oh, never mind all that.

This is the embarrassing part. After complaining
so vociferously about the eggs I went to pay my bill

and discovered I had no money with me
so I had to go home and get my wallet
and bring it back to the restaurant
making myself a liar for having said
this is it, I'm never coming back.
The waitress was very nice about it all.

Is it hard to write poetry?
Yes, I would say it is. For instance
in this poem I didn't know whether to start
by talking about the scrambled eggs
or the Smith Corona. And I didn't have
a lot of time to think about it
because I simply had to start the poem,
it was that urgent,
and then you have to torture yourself
wondering if it's all right to write about
writing in a poem and you keep resolving
never again to write about writing
and you always break your resolve.
It's as if writing has a will of its own
and wants to be written about
just like Margaret Hollingsworth's
typewriter.

# Mickey Mouse

When I was a kid I looked through a keyhole and thought I saw Mickey Mouse. After that, whenever I was in the vicinity of that particular keyhole I would look through, hoping to see Mickey Mouse again. But he never reappeared. It took several months before I gave up, sad because the natural visionary ability of childhood was beginning to fade.

On Monday I told you I would be staring at you from a distance on Tuesday. On Tuesday I looked through the window of the bank and saw you talking to the manager. You looked over your shoulder at me. On Wednesday you wrote a poem in which this incident was mentioned. On Thursday you mailed me the poem. On Friday I received it. On Saturday I walked past the bank and looked through the window but no one was there.

On Saturday when I got home my house was full of fruit and camera equipment. The note said you had gone looking for Easter eggs in the tall grass (this was October) and you had found all these zucchinis, squashes, vegetable marrows, apples, pears, plums, tripods, zoom lenses, light meters.

It's midnight. I'm alone. In the distance a dog is barking. I am wondering about that vision of Mickey Mouse. My head is sweet with the taste of the plums.

## Stormy January

### I

It is as if I had an eye on the side of my head
just in front of my left ear
and when I turn away from the window
I can still see the falling snow.
The universe is a small place
the size of a booby-trapped toy
(coincidence can kill you). Somehow
it's right that it should snow in January.
No one ever commits suicide during a snowstorm
except for Frank Sinatra in *Young at Heart*.
As I write this I am wearing black socks,
a wine Picasso sweatshirt and blue cords.

Yesterday I met a Jungian who only wanted to talk
about Richard Strauss's influence on Norval Morrisseau.
The man worked as a public relations officer for the ministry
of health and was wearing a Kennedy Space Centre T-shirt.
He disagreed when I told him Stanley Kubrick's 2001
was a remake of Walt Disney's *Fantasia*. Nothing I could
say would make him laugh. I told him my mother was Japanese
but I became disoriented. I spoke of the perfume machine
being out of odour. I spoke of a world of parallel structures,
pigs' ears, mountains with snowy peaks, pyramids, television.
He wasn't even interested when I told him Marjorie had her
hysterectomy on the same day Frank and Mona became lovers.

### II

When Marjorie got home from the hospital she painted
a picture of herself being struck by lightning.
Months later when Mona became pregnant and Frank
realized his mistake and tried to get back with Marjorie
Marjorie had fallen in love with Jed.

## III

Jed had been waiting for Anne to return from Fiji.
Which brings me to my reason for writing.
Anne is expected back from Fiji today.
Canada in January is no place for political
slogans: everything there exists within
a giant spiritual eye as soft as moonlight.
Sometimes I sit in the park and let the snow
pile up around me. The salamander survives the flames
but doesn't necessarily enjoy the experience.
When we are young there are certain people
we know are brighter than we, people who can
exploit their experience in more courageous ways.
When we are older we see we have outlived these people.
They've gone mad and destroyed themselves.

Marx of weakness, marx of woe.
When I turn my head away from the window
I can still see Picasso shrouded in snow.

Sometimes I think I am an eye. At other times, no.


## IV

Jim was a painter and a trumpet player, a passionate
drunk who accused everyone of having a Picasso
complex and devised dozens of devious ways
of getting Free Booze. He had grounds privileges
at the psychiatric hospital. One night he was late
returning and was locked out. They found his body
at the foot of the escarpment in the morning.
And we wonder at our own lack of courage. We see *High Noon*
and we know we would have joined that posse.
But still we wonder at that urge to survive,
that urge that comes from the flames below,
and we wonder why the angels do not give to others
the same comfort and protection they give to us,
and we wonder at other old friends, successful people
with houses and families, old friends
who do not enjoy anything about their lives,

and we pray to the angels to go to the assistance
of these others but the angels refuse, radiantly.


V


Your political friends will encourage you to forget
the sacredness of the individual baby lamb.
Where the Kootenay and the Columbia rivers finally meet
there is simply silence. I dreamt I was lonely
and I dreamt someone told my mother I wanted
to return to Ontario. The sources of both rivers
are a few miles apart in the Rocky Mountains
but the Kootenay flows north for a thousand miles
and the Columbia south, and when they meet
(just outside my window) there is only silence.
Except for last night when a man, a woman and a baby lamb
appeared (just outside my window). The man
said he'd recently returned from Australia and the woman
said that's a long way from there to here.
She'd just returned from Mexico and he said
did you drink the water? And she said no,
I just drank mescal. It was nice to be home,
thinking of Pablo Picasso again. And they argued
about dams, dams on the Columbia and Kootenay rivers,
and he said he never saw a dam he didn't like
and she said but dams are ugly and dams damn rivers!
Actually, I quite like McFadden's work.

And the lamb began to speak and said I'd been
in Buddhaland long enough. The Great Cosmic Buddha
wanted you here for some reason and now it wants you
to return, it said. It was as if I had an eye
on the side of my head just in front of my ear.
Everyone was wearing Kennedy Space Centre T-shirts that year.
And sometimes I get flashes of the man
I would have been had I been born in another century.
This man is inside me, I can feel him, a happy man,
kind, natural, full of humour and innocence.
He doesn't have hot wires running through his mind
nor does he have steel plates nailed to his flesh.

I can feel his warmth, the rise and fall
of his breath, and his sadness when I manifest
aspects of my severely damaged personality.

But that's enough political sloganeering.


## VI

In the centre of the universe a pair of baby lambs
wrestle in the grass, and there are crocuses,
and bluebells, and drops of dew on every blade,
and there is a cow in the distance, and there is
a plane, a DC-3, flying over the hill.

There's a full moon as we sail into the lagoon
somewhere south of Fiji. Behind us is the forest
thick with snakes and vines and hints of volcanoes.
Random lambs, each shining with a light of its own,
stand on branches of trees. Huge star-shaped diamonds
hover over our heads. The lambs are staring up at them.
We are full of devotion. Somewhere a woman has just been
told her children have been murdered.
In the centre of the universe is a lamb.


## VII

People say to me all the time, they say, Norval
(for that's my name), are you a Jungian?
And I always tell them that when Picasso
died, his spirit entered my body
and there it has remained, and I
don't have to be anything but myself.
And I tell them my mind does not tolerate even its own
systems of thought and experience, nor does it
enjoy its eternal life among the flames
for it is a jealous little mind
that feeds on neo-Platonism and art,
knowledge with which to destroy the minds of others,
and it is anxious for me to die
so that it can enter the minds of others
and destroy them even more completely,

and I'd do anything for it, just anything
and it knows it. Those who can read
can read my autobiography in these paintings,
the story of my flirtations with systematic destruction,
the story of my experiments in trying to discover
what I'd be like in different time frames
with no Third Reich monkey a more or less
permanent resident of my rib cage,
the story of my attempts to track down the lambs
who are said to be wrestling at the centre of the universe,
the story of my attempts to illuminate
in my paintings my own life and the lives
of those who do not want their lives illuminated.

I know I talk a lot but
in a secret ceremony the angels
have made me a priest of light.
The kind of light that is the same as
darkness, a mechanical light,
a night of endless radiance
that animates the universe like the spring
in a little waxwork dummy of Picasso.
My painting is a rocketship to heaven.
My images are cut from the trunks
of living trees. There are no phantoms
in these condensors of memory,
no sense of an unattainable reality.
There are no symbols, for as soon
as you decipher the symbols something
dies, an existential integrity.
"To one madness we oppose another."
The most perverse are the innocent
and nature no longer interests even them.
When we are young we are told only the
dull can be content. So we torment
ourselves to demonstrate our intelligence.
We forget to keep our eye on the puck,
your perfect mechanical lamb.

To sum up, only life in the twentieth century
can bring you true peace of mind.

## Pat Lowther

The mind is a clear sky with light to heavy
traffic and occasional mid-air collisions.
Joggers are jogging by on Bedford Road.
A large stray cat is walking up the alley
towards my window. A small black cat
with violet collar leaps on the stray;
they both snarl and paw. The stray
keeps its ground, the violet collar withdraws.
On the ground floor of the brown brick house
to the south of the alley a prominent lawyer
is eating a breakfast of sausage and pancakes.
On the second floor of the white brick house
to the north of the alley a woman is screaming.
For at least two weeks her husband has been doing
nothing but watching television.
She is screaming about madness and divorce.
I can see him sitting there in front of the TV
holding his head in agony.
She is standing over him, screaming.
The Buddhists say the chances of being born human
are as slim as a turtle in the vast sea
accidentally surfacing inside an inner tube.
That is why they sit around meditating,
allowing the mind to glow like a planet.
It is a rare privilege to be born human.
When she saw the hate in his eyes and the rock
       in his hand
the beautiful poet about to be murdered
pictured herself at home, in front of the TV,
a friendly cat named Oscar sitting on her lap.

# Dreary Weekend at Halfmoon Bay

Far out on the horizon the sun has broken through
and a series of shafts of varying degrees of brightness
is illuminating islands so small in the distance
they look like flecks of fingernail dirt
and life is so unutterably sad
my heart feels like a big piece
of some kind of cheese I don't like.

And now the sun is picking up
a range of strangely shaped clouds:
the snow-capped mountains of Vancouver Island.

And the seabirds in pairs with sad spontaneity
remind me of my lack of imagination,
and the sad symphony of the songbirds of the forest
remind me that I'll never be
as intelligent as I want to be,
and the eagles with their huge wings
remind me I'm getting old and the sad
memories of my childhood have all faded.

If I were to shoot myself now
my body would fall to the floor of this leaky cabin
but my soul would continue hanging here
for centuries like a dim lightbulb
or a large single eye with cataract
trying to figure out where it went wrong.

# White Dog

The white dog
ran across the white snow
under a full moon

then turned
and looked back

towards the house
where I stood
watching it out the kitchen window

a cat sleeping in my arms
my heart shining.

## Bev and Dwight

Bev was showing her slides from Mexico
and there was one of Dwight
hitting himself on the head
with a yellow flower.

And so I said to Dwight
who has plenty of intellectual power
why are you hitting yourself on the head
with a yellow flower?

And before he could answer Bev said
he saw some Mexicans each of whom
was hitting himself on the head
with a yellow flower

and he wanted to see what would happen
if he
hit himself on the head
with a yellow flower.

I was an ethnographer at the time,
said Dwight, and I'd try anything,
and so he hit himself on the head
with a yellow flower.

And I could tell by the look in his eye
that nothing happened
when he hit himself on the head
with a yellow flower.

## Adults at Play

Sunny winter morning in Nelson, B.C.
I say hello to my bird
and she cheeps back at me.
On the street I ask a kid
what's the name of your dog?
(It's a white cairn terrier.)
It's not my dog, says the kid, it's a neighbour's.

Last night a plane bound for Florida
crashed into the Fourteenth Street bridge in
Washington, D.C.
And there was a traffic jam on the bridge
and all the motorists were killed.
The plane landed in the frozen Potomac
with all kinds of heroic rescue attempts,
people diving off what was left of the bridge
to save people they didn't even know,
helicopter pilots risking their lives and all that.
And at the same time in the same city
two subway trains crashed head-on
and another bunch of people were killed.
Urban synchronicity.

Anyway, I smiled at the kid with the
cairn terrier and got on the bus.
There was a sign saying adults thirty-five cents,
children ten cents.
So I put in a dime and said to the driver
that's for the child in me
then I put in a quarter and said to the driver
and that's for the adult in me.
And the driver
who on most days seems friendly
looked at me as if I'd been shouting
subversive slogans
and his face was all red
and his neck.

And so I am thinking of having a sign printed up
a sign that could be posted at the front of every bus
in the entire eight-bus Nelson public transit system:

Please don't say anything to the driver
that might cause him to have to shift gears
mentally.

# Serenity and Posterity

My grandmother is cutting my nails and telling me
that she can remember *her* grandmother cutting *her* nails
and it always made her fingertips feel naked
for the rest of the day,
I write in the present of a memory thirty years old.

My grandmother sat in her armchair all day
reading her Bible and serenity rose
from her body like bouquets of roses
and if anyone said anything
her head would turn slowly with a smile.

Her name was Celeste Dunsmoor, she was born
to a pioneer family in Rocky Saugeen, her father
was deaf and was killed by a train
while pulling home a sleigh full of wood.

On the radio an announcer talks about Mendelssohn:
"When you are able to combine lyricism with serenity
you are able to leave a message for posterity
that will not soon be forgotten."

## Oscar Wilde

Quite often I would stand on the ridge
watching the sun set into the sea on the one side
and the full moon rise out of the sea on the other
and arguing with myself about the nature
of truth. I knew nothing of global politics
but I knew that when I told a lie everyone believed me
and when I told the truth they turned away in disbelief
and so I asked Oscar Wilde what I should do
about this conspiracy of silence surrounding me
and he said join it. He said I know you
but I do not know where I know you from.

# The Hunchback

All summer my dog has had skin problems, the fur falling from his back, the skin raw. But now that the cool weather is finally here the skin has healed and the fur is growing.

And the leaves have fallen from the trees and are heaped on the ground. The sky is all colours, but mostly grey.

Roy Kiyooka says as an artist he's responsible for putting images in the world, images which if they were not there would be somehow missed. And nobody else can put them there.

He speaks of being obsessed with the shapeliness of the day.

And I think of my dog growing old and I open the door and he comes bounding in out of the cold. His hair is all grown back.

A month ago my dog and I were standing with a group of people at a point where a fast-flowing stream flowed into a lake. A polar bear came floating by and the people were alarmed. They feared the bear would drown. So one of the men jumped into the water and captured the bear and placed him in a cage.

My dog was almost uncontrollable. He was growling and puffing himself up, and I could hardly keep a grip on his leash.

It didn't seem right to me that something so beautiful should be in a cage. But it was for the bear's own protection. No one could figure how the bear had got this far south.

Then a strange thing happened. One of the children somehow managed to climb into the cage. And although the bear didn't make a move to harm the child, the parents began screaming.

The same man who'd captured the bear entered the cage and brought out the child unharmed. The bear just sat there unconcerned, all through the rescue attempt. But once the child was out of the cage, the bear began biting the bars and growling. His pink nose looked like the nipple of a pregnant woman.

Someone once said the job of a writer is to give a point to that which is pointless. But the only point to this story is that it happened at a certain time, a certain place, like a hunchback leaping from the roof of a cathedral.

Beyond that all we can do is listen to our hearts beating.

# Tibetan Mandala

I told him of my dream of being a member of a tribe
of Indians. I'm given a large round wooden shield
brightly painted and told to go out into the battlefield
with nothing but the shield and ward off an entire
European invasion. I decide I'm certainly going to die
but the shield which strongly resembles a Tibetan mandala
renders the total European arsenal ineffective.

That is a powerful dream, he said.
He said he too had one the night before.
He had fuzzy hair like an African's
and he was walking inside a Tibetan monastery
and a holy man said he should do more chanting
and so he woke up and chanted for three hours.

And he spoke of a certain kind of meditation
where you breathe in, in the form of a black fog,
all the suffering of all the world, and let it disappear
into your heart. And when you do so, he said,
all your self-cherishing and grasping disappears as well.
And you breathe out, in the form of a white light
coming up out of your heart out into all
the ten directions of space, a white light, he said,
which represents the essence of love and brings
joy and peace to every sentient being.
This is a very profound meditation, he said.
And he smiled and said Chuggy teaches it too.

He counselled me against meditating on emptiness
for that is too intellectual a practice, he said.
Better, he said, to meditate on the essential
dependency of the individual. Even better, he said,
is to meditate on merely subduing self-cherishing,
ridding yourself of thoughts of ego as they arise.
Stronger still, he said, is the practice
of subduing the mind itself. And he spoke

of the ninth-century poet Shantideva's concept
of the mind as a wild elephant that has to be bound.

He was leaving for Toronto, via Lake Louise, in the morning,
and he wouldn't be back for two months.
We sipped tea, he gave me two pictures of himself
and I gave him Jack's address in Toronto.
And we embraced and I left.

# Margaret Hollingsworth's Milk

Margaret Hollingsworth phones you first thing in the morning
and asks if you'll bring her a jug of two per cent
when you come up the hill to the college
because she has torn ligaments from a skiing accident
Saturday and you are happy to oblige
but when you hang up you remember it'll be impossible
for you to get to her place for a couple of hours
at least and you can't phone her back to tell her
because you don't want to put her through the misery
of hobbling to the phone for what might after all
be a rather insignificant (to her) message
so you don't phone

but by the time you arrive at her door
a couple of hours later with the milk
after going to the bank to see about an NSF cheque
to the *Nelson Daily News* to see about the magazine
to the flower shop to order some pink roses
for your mother who is in the hospital

she is sitting there at the kitchen table
right next to the telephone
her left leg all wrapped up
and you could have called after all
but she smiles anyway
and says thank you
and says it doesn't matter the milk is late

and you look out the window at the clouds
sailing in over the crest of Elephant Mountain

as you always do at Margaret Hollingsworth's place.

## Love's Golden Splendor

A woman is reading a book called *Love's Golden Splendor*
on the bus heading down to the Pape station
and I look out the window and see a young man
pushing an old lady in a wheelchair, quickly,
for it is about to start raining.
Later, on the subway, there's another woman
reading *Love's Golden Splendor*, and a young
African woman, fashionably dressed, sits by herself
unselfconsciously singing Billie Holiday songs.

My verses are subtle yet unschooled, amateur but never
didactic. The twentieth century means nothing to me.
This could be ninth-century China for all I care.
Everything is myth. I've wound up all my affairs
and am about to put all my possessions in a boat
and push it out in the bay and sink it. We have never
taken a step out of eternity. I think it's time
for you to come with me. Let's just go
and let's not know or even care where we're going.

# The Armadillo

A woman I hadn't seen in years
phoned today to say she'd come home
and found an armadillo in her kitchen
a live armadillo
quietly eating from the cat's bowl

and it had a collar around its neck
and attached to the collar
was a tag
with my name on it

What's going on?
she said

and I answered
truthfully
I knew nothing about it.

## Work Poem

He was carrying a stack of boxes so heavy
it looked as if they were full of lead.
His spine was bent, his eyes bulging
and sweat was running down his nose.

"Excuse me, my friend," I said, unwrapping
an expensive Havana cigar. "Could I
bother you for a light?" He stopped,
put down his boxes with a groan

and pulled out a book of matches. "No,"
I said, "I was just fooling. I'm sorry.
I just wanted to see what you'd say. Forgive me."
He was wearing a sweatshirt with the slogan

TAKE CARE OF ME I'M HARD TO REPLACE.
"Well, make up your mind," he said, and he picked up
his stack of boxes, groaned again
and continued staggering down the street.

# Annie and Ian

## I

Annie knew she was pregnant
and kept getting more and more frustrated
when her doctor kept telling her she wasn't.

Annie lived way up in the mountains
with her two little girls
and her husband Ian
and their two golden retrievers

and it wasn't easy to change doctors.

One night Annie slipped on the ice
and aborted the baby right there on the driveway.
It was a Saturday night so she and Ian
stashed the baby in the freezer for the weekend.

On Monday Annie stomped into the doctor's office
and clunked the frozen baby down on his desk.
Now tell me I wasn't pregnant, she said.

## II

The golden retrievers had been litter mates
and had never been apart, their names
were Cedar and Major.

Cedar developed some kind of infection
and didn't respond to treatment.
She continued lying there wagging her tail
as the vet took Ian aside and said he'd done
all he could and suggested he take her home
for the night and bring her back in the morning
and they'd put her down.

In the morning Ian made Cedar her favourite
breakfast, bacon and eggs. She gobbled them down
then barfed them up.
And continued bleeding from the mouth.

So Ian took Cedar to the vet's and the vet
stuck the needle in. Cedar sniffed it
then sighed and fell asleep.

Ian put the body in the trunk and called Major over.
Major went into shock.

Ian drove into the woods, found a spot, dug a grave.
It had to be a big grave because Cedar was a big dog.
He wrapped Cedar in a sheet and lowered her down.
Ian was a Zen Buddhist so he put a gold Buddha in with her
and lit three sticks of incense: one for the sangha,
one for the dharma, and one for the Buddha.

Ian meditated by the side of the grave.
Major meditated too, his head in Ian's lap.
Both of them cried for a while
then went home and watched the Super Bowl.

Problem: Terry was staying at Annie and Ian's
while his wife was in the hospital dying of cancer.
She was due to die any day and Terry
was terribly upset.

Terry kept making fun of Ian for being so sad
about the death of a mere dog.
So Annie finally got mad
and Terry left
and never came back.

## Crossing Second Narrows Bridge
## in an Old Blue Morris Minor

The Japanese ship that was being loaded with lumber all last week
under the Second Narrows Bridge
has gone and is somewhere out in the Pacific now.
This is the same bridge that collapsed
during construction in 1959,
the same year this old car was built,
and perhaps the car came off the assembly line in Britain
on the same day twenty-three workers fell to their cursed deaths
in the twisted metal of Burrard Inlet.

And now you can see the little wooden houses
around the end of the bridge
and you try to hear that horrendous crash
of two decades ago
and you try to realize the sudden shock of a huge bridge
collapsing before your eyes
on a day otherwise
much like any other.

Memories are made of this,
and today driving over the bridge I pick my nose
and in the pickup truck driving alongside
three guys stare at me.

Sometimes something you're making collapses
before you're finished, other times
everything goes right and you know
it'll hold up forever. And what you know
will hold up forever is often indistinguishable
from that which is about to collapse.
The difference is something deeply buried
like twenty-three embarrassing corpses
whose names are dutifully inscribed
on an undated plaque at the foot of the bridge.

It's all a matter of intent, like the Mexican

railroad in *Under the Volcano* — excessively curved
because the workers were getting paid by the mile,
and it's often said of a winding river
it's being paid by the mile.

And the bogus bridge-builders are all around us.
It's no longer worthwhile to build a good bridge
unless you do it so furtively
no one will know what you're doing.

## Letter to My Father

In the past couple of years my life has become
incredibly trivial. I have become what they call
a creative writing instructor in a small college in the interior
of British Columbia. I paste on my office door, to compensate,
serious pictures — the Beheading of John the Baptist,
news photos of political executions, tortured bodies,
racing cars going out of control and flying into the crowd —
and students are annoyed or maybe the security guards or
        cleaning staff
for when I arrive in the morning the pictures have been torn
        down.
The students want to know how to become poets, how to write
        poems.
I tell them to think of a line, any line, and write it down.
Something like this: A Zimbabwe farmer, following the
        revolution,
says his "moral" has been destroyed because he no longer has
        anything
to live for. Then think of another line and write it down.
Something like: Father, what's it like to be old? And if
these two lines suggest a third put that down too, and a fourth,
and a fifth, as long as you're not forcing your mind to be
involved in what you're doing. And I genuinely like these people.
That's what amazes me, my feeling for them as individuals,
but they complain about me: tell me I'm obsessed
with form, that I ignore content, that I'm unable to appreciate
their individual vision, that I'm an old windbag.
Yeah, to them I'm an old guy. Your little boy has become old
at least in the eyes of the younger students. Others, older,
have given me their hearts, a more than fair exchange,
and last month as my fortieth birthday came closer
I started to panic. I even thought of walking out, walking out
to the end of the Government Wharf with a shotgun
and blowing my head out over the cold waters of Kootenay Lake
so that people would say gee he killed himself on his fortieth
birthday and people would say *tsk* I guess he feared old age.
Don't be alarmed. I learned this from you. You know

my childhood memories are full of images of you as a
warm, soft, likable (I had to check the spelling, you always
said don't ever write a word until you know how to spell it),
witty, moral, and highly selfconscious individual. The only
sport you took an interest in was boxing, or pugilistics
as your father used to say. You were my model in every way
and today the image I have of myself is almost identical
to the image of you I had as a child.
But you never had illusions about humanity. You told me
never to allow myself to be fingerprinted
and never to put anything in a letter I didn't want
the whole world to know. Oh my!
And I remember the sad look that came in your eye
when I in my high chair flicked a spoonful of Pablum
into your face, that face that now is my own, the same look
when twelve years later we sadly tossed Uncle Joe's photos
into the fire. For you life was wonderful
but individual human beings were not so wonderful.
Maybe that's what you meant when you told me the whole
is greater than the sum of its parts. Mind over matter.

And, father, do you remember the time you dropped the monkey
wrench on your toe? I guess your foot was bare, the wrench fell
from the top of the furnace, you were very brave,
I don't remember you crying or yelling, ever,
though I remember you sad lots of times.
So your foot was an awful mess, the doctor came
and bandaged it up, and as for me it seemed right somehow
that my father should drop a monkey wrench on his foot.
That was the sort of thing that adults do.

When you were my age I was sixteen, almost as old
as some of my students. And I imagine they see me much as I
saw you. Probably not true but you have to believe something
unless you want to dissolve into the universe, honey into honey.
I was discussing astrology and one of the students
said she was born under the sign of Aquarius and I told her
both my parents were Aquarians. She looked surprised
and said I bet you never get along with them. On the contrary,
I said, I love them very much and consider it a tragedy
I live so far from them and seldom see them particularly

now when they're getting on in years, although it's true
their lives are harmonious, they're in good health, and don't
really need me. You know me. My needs are small. I go where I think
I might be needed. And sometimes I feel needed here.
For eighteen years I saw you every day. For the next eighteen
I saw you every Sunday. And now I see you once or twice a year.
Some day, maybe soon, we'll be permanently separated by death.
But both of us know there is no death,
just as there is no life, there is only us,
all together, all the time, for all eternity,
in a kind of incredibly intelligent and compassionate light
which is for now just outside our little minds.

Father, I know little of your sorrows, your fears,
although I know you have your share of them.
But as much as one human being can care for another human being
I will always care for you.

# Kitsilano Beach on a May Evening

If you told them you wanted to be a fireman some day
they'd let you in to watch the big game on television
at the Kenilworth Avenue firehall in 1954
and you'd ride your bicycle along the Pipe Line
past the row of wooden posts painted green and see
the blossoming pear tree in her back yard and she'd
be there, sunning, reading *The Old Man and the Sea,*
on the back-porch roof, in her green bikini.

When does the possibility of taking one's own life
first appear? You'd ask for her brother,
a few years older, long wavy blond hair, blue eyes
that never seemed to look at you or anyone.
And she'd say he's gone, gone to Hollywood
to be a movie star, and you'd say you'd seen a movie
and the star reminded you of her, and she'd say
she hated that movie and was insulted that you
thought she resembled such a third-rate actress
and she was pink in the spring, brown in the summer,
grey in the fall and white in the winter,
Ruth was her name, hair the colour of daffodils,
and nothing came of your desire to befriend her.
Years later you heard she'd been convicted of stealing
money from the bank where she worked as a teller
and giving it to her boyfriend to buy heroin.

And you remember the night when you were eight.
You'd just finished reading Peter Pan for the eighth time
and for the eighth time felt a wave of embarrassment.
There was a pregnant woman walking by under the streetlamps.
You punched her in the stomach full force and ran home.
And the time your friend Bobby Zambori
in short pants was sitting on the front step,
your dad scraping the house for paint.
You held the tip of a screwdriver in the flame
of the blowtorch for several minutes
then touched it to Bobby's bare leg.

You've always been psychotic. You always look
as if you've just finished strangling a cat.
Just last year you deserted your wife and children
with particular cruelty. You enjoy thinking about it.
And you're glad you thought to put on a sweater
on this cool spring evening in the strange orange light
of Kitsilano Beach, your slow lazy breathing
cooling your heart's excessive heat.

Lonely men stroll by and glance at you. They are wondering
what you're thinking, walking so slow. Two mallards
float by on the oil-slicked swells of English Bay. A young
blonde woman sits on a bench under a light. She is reading
*The Old Man and the Sea*. Several freighters
are moored farther out. Dozens of grapefruit
bob up and down in the water. Maybe they've fallen
from one of the boats. Maybe they're full of heroin!
The lights and outline of a large sailboat sailing slowly
in towards False Creek Mouth remind you of wealth and poverty.
The old steam locomotive in the park reminds you of Chiang's
soldiers who used to take captives and shove them live
down the chimneys of locomotives like this, down into
the steam chambers full of boiling water.

Suddenly you hear a scream, a girl's voice.
She yells out "No!" as if she really means it.
It seems to have come from the dark area behind the
tennis courts and you search through clumps of trees
and find nothing. Don't bother calling a cop.
They'd never take you seriously. Besides,
how do you know you didn't imagine the voice?
Don't you still sometimes hear your mother calling you?

Remember that photo you sent your mother last year?
You wrote on the back here's the nicest person in the world
saying hello to all the other nice people in the world.
And of course you meant it, even though now
you've taken to warning people what a rotten bastard you are,
how you love to betray people when they've finally
yielded their absolute vulnerability, how you'd be shot
in wartime and probably will be even in peacetime.
You wouldn't last a day in Belfast or Beirut.

And then you begin to preen, speaking in the most
superficial Jungian terms of the shadow's integration
and when your naïve audience asks what you do with it
once it's integrated you say you keep your eye on it
like a lama measuring his breathing in and out
for once you're aware of your capacity for monstrosity
you're less likely to destroy yourself and others
and all you want to do is live in peace, by yourself,
adding nothing to the misery of the world.
That black hump over there is Stanley Park.
That incongruous constellation of stars is the illuminated
Grouse Mountain ski lift. Two men are standing
on the breakwater scooping the grapefruit with butterfly nets.
Everything that ever was is in the air tonight.
On the horizon, tug-boat operators are getting drunk.

With a tender smile you draw Ruth towards you and touch
your lips to her forehead so impossibly chaste and lovely.
She is wearing nothing but a loincloth.
She is fourteen forever.

# Frank O'Hara

It was the high-school orchestra. We raised money
by selling aluminum clothes-peg boxes.
On the side of each was a red emblem.
I think it said REALISTIC.
You can check it out. There are still some
nailed to posts in the east end of Hamilton, Ontario.
And with the money we went on an Easter field trip
to New York.
The music teacher
Bernard Blades
fell in love with the string-bass player
Lois Lawrence.
She must have been sixteen.
He left his wife and kids
and married her.
Actually he stole her away from the trombone player
who was also sixteen.
This kind of thing never happens in Archie.
The trombone player I met years later
and he told me that Mr. Blades and Lois
had been very happy
for a while
and had a couple of kids of their own
but in her early thirties Lois got cancer
and died
and two weeks later Mr. Blades had a heart attack
and died.
I thought the trombone player sounded a little smug,
as if he were happy the way it turned out.
He belonged to one of those funny religions.
Seventh Day Adventists?

Meanwhile, back in New York, I didn't want to go
to the United Nations building
so I sneaked off to the Museum of Modern Art
which wasn't on our itinerary
and got into a long interesting conversation

with the man at the Information Counter.
He was so nice to me and he took me for a Coke
and paid for it himself
and he knew all about poetry and art
and he even said Jack Kerouac and William Burroughs
were friends of his
and he told me it was very important never to let yourself
get bored by poetry
if you wanted to keep writing
and he advised me to stay in Canada
and give up my desire
to move to New York when I turned eighteen.
Years later I read the poetry of Frank O'Hara
and when I saw his picture
I knew
that's who it had been.

And now Frank too
along with Mr. Blades and Lois
is dead
but I bet Frank at any rate
is not bored
not even by this poem.
Are you, Frank?

# The Deer Hunter

At the back of the sporting goods store
was an old poster advertising hunting rifles
and showing a deer standing there
between the campfire and the tent
and a man running madly for his rifle
his pants down around his knees
a roll of toilet paper
unwinding behind him.

We were driving to Spokane
along a slow ice-covered winding mountain road
and a large brown dog
ran out of the woods
and it looked as if it were going
to run into the path of the car
and I swerved
and went off the road
and rolled the car
which came to rest
an inch from a thousand-foot drop.

Your head was bleeding.
You said I was crazy
for swerving to avoid a mere dog.

And I said
I thought it was a deer
which was true.

# The Rat

I am taking care of Virginia
while her mother attends summer school
and over the radio comes the news
that deadly disease-carrying rats
have invaded the lower Muskokas.

Then a rat
with a human-looking face
darts past the cottage
and I turn to see Virginia
writhing on the ground.

I look again and she's dead.

I take off with a knife.
I hope to catch the rat and kill it
before it kills others.

It runs into a crowded store
and I manage to corner it
and pounce on it
and I hold its teeth away from my arms
by pressing the knife against its neck
and as I hesitate
the rat turns into a young girl
about twelve
extremely frightened.

I begin hacking at her neck
until long streams of blood begin spurting
and soon she is dead

and when I look up
dozens of people are staring at me
with horrified faces.

To them I've just murdered
an innocent child.

# Negative Ions

Whenever I have a lot of heavy reading to do
I like to sit at the table closest to the Suzuki fountain
on the main floor of the Metro library on Yonge Street
for the negative ions from the fountain keep me awake
and I place my special three-dimensional Xograph postcard
featuring the picture of Jesus superimposed
on the picture of the Turin Shroud
on the table
so that no one will bother me
and I'm never bothered. This could almost be you
writing this poem.

                    And today, sitting there, reading,
I became more and more startled by a memory that appeared
displaced in time. It was a memory of you and me,
sitting at a table in front of the bandstand at the
Town Casino in Buffalo, and we were drinking beer
and listening to Miles Davis and his Quintet,
and Herbie Hancock on piano was only seventeen years old
and Miles announced that it was Herbie's first date
and you and I smiled shyly because it was our first date
and everyone could tell Herbie Hancock was going to be
famous on his own, too strong to be a sideman forever,
and every now and then I noticed Miles staring at you
admiringly, and there was hardly anyone in the Town Casino,
Miles wasn't the big name he is now, just a few folks there,
drinking beer, and Miles and the band showed up an hour late
and the manager was upset and said where the hell were you
and Miles said, unapologetically, they couldn't tear themselves
away from the TV football game in their hotel, they were annoyed
because the owner was such a redneck, behind the bandstand
was a mural showing darkies picking cotton.

It felt as if this event had happened last week
but I knew it had happened a lifetime ago,
a bullet out of the past entering my head
and killing me with the sadness of the passing of time,

and I was startled and disoriented, it was as if
an elemental pair of wires had crossed in my mind,
viewing the same memory from a pair of points in time,
and I thought of phoning you and asking if you remembered
that Sunday afternoon so long ago and if you remembered it
with any particular clarity but I didn't
because I didn't want to do anything
that would make you sad,
you haven't been well lately.

And I started writing all this down and after a while
I noticed with a start that I was writing it
in your handwriting.

And I stopped writing and I could hear the fountain again
like rain on the roof of a cabin in the woods,
vacant cabin,
empty woods,

and all of this could have happened to you, and if
it had you might have written this poem.

# A Sentimental Introduction

Everyday I sit for two hours
removing the poison from the ozone
and replacing it with spiritual light

so that people on the street below
will sometimes look up at my window
and smile, for I am a sponge
in the bath of urban life,
and there is a neutrality about me
right down to the question mark that sits
throbbing like blue neon in my pancreas
and people who get close to me
say there's nothing to like, nothing to dislike.
Being with me is like eating plain yogurt.
I'm as lovable as an ion generator.

And this morning as I lay sleeping
the sun shone through my window
so that I dreamt I was in a snowstorm
and eating vanilla ice cream
then I walked down to the beach
where people were swimming and sunbathing
and when I awoke a pigeon flew through the window
and left a white mess in my coffee
then sat there criticizing me
for not ending my poems properly

and I told it the movie last night
was so good I couldn't take a moment
to go for a pee so I peed
in my empty popcorn container
and when I got thirsty I likewise
couldn't leave to get a drink
and so I drank the piss —
Too bad you weren't there, I said,
you could have had some,

and it flew away.

# A Cup of Tea with Issa

I've never seen a raindrop fall on a frog's head but you have. You say the frog wiped away the water with his wrist and that's good enough for me.

Ever since I first heard it fifteen years ago your poem on the death of your son has been flitting in and out of my mind. And now I see there are two versions, the first having been revised on the later death of your daughter, in 1819, of smallpox. And now I want you to know that I hope you've been reunited with your sons and your daughters and your wives and your father, and that I prefer the first version.

The sun has dropped behind the mountains and the tiny cars on the long winding road way over on the other side of the lake have their lights on. And a sense of amazement springs up, amazement that we live in a world where the sun continually rises and sets.

The *Marismius oreades* (delicious when fried with bacon) have formed a fairy ring in the shape of a giant number 3 in the courtyard lawn, reminding me of the time I saw three motorcycles parked diagonally at the curb in front of 111 Brucedale Avenue.

In October you can look at the sides of the mountains and see the patterns made by the deciduous trees which have become bright yellow or orange among the coniferous which have remained dark green. Sometimes it seems like a territorial war up there but the conflict between the two types of trees is probably more in my mind than on the slopes.

This morning the sky is blue but the tops of the mountains cling to thick giant puffs of pink and grey cloud. A small white cloud rises from the surface of the lake and tries to reach the big ones up above but by the time it gets half way there it has almost completely disappeared.

It's pleasant to be so unhurried that you can see even the slowest-moving clouds moving. A part of me says I should be ashamed of myself but you know the more time you waste the more you get. It's like money.

On a rainy windy October morning a grey Volkswagen sits at the side of the road. It's covered with hundreds of small wet yellow leaves plastered on the trunk, on the hood, on the roof — in a strangely satisfying pattern. Was it the rain and the wind or was it an incredibly subtle and patient artist with a pot of glue? Of course it was the wind and the rain and of course this is a hackneyed idea. But for a moment I wonder. As you would have.

It's pleasant to have a cup of tea and think of you, Issa, and to think of others in the twentieth century having a cup of tea and thinking of you, Issa.

# Tibetan Monologue

When you're driving along a winding mountain road
during a blizzard
and a transport truck passes you
splattering slush all over your windshield
and causing you to go out of control
and roll over in the ditch
the driver of the truck
was your father in a previous incarnation.

When you're getting loaded
in a sleazy bar on Davie Street
and a fourteen-year-old in spike boots
and a pink mohair sweater
asks you if you want a blow job
and you ask how much
and she says two bucks
that girl
was your mother in a previous incarnation.

When you're flying over British Columbia
in a Pacific Western Boeing 747
and you've got a head cold and your
Eustachian tubes are all plugged up
and the pressure is getting more and more intense
and soon you're holding your head in agony
even screaming
and your eardrums are forming bubbles
like thin membranes of bubblegum
and your eyes are bulging
like Halloween candy apples
with razor blades in them
and you're just going crazy for the plane to land
and the pilot announces that the plane won't be landing
at Castlegar
because of fog conditions
it will have to go on to Cranbrook
and an hour later the pilot announces

they can't land at Cranbrook either
and they're going to turn around and fly back
to Vancouver
and see if they might be able to land there
and you're screaming for help
and everyone is ignoring you
because there's nothing they can do anyway
everybody was your mom and dad
in previous incarnations.

# Dick the Amateur Gardener

It's raining today, the rain is filling
all the little tubes in the earth. If there
is a rabbit hole, the rainwater is pouring in,
and I wonder if that pop singer of the fifties,
Marvin Rainwater, is still alive, and if he is,
if it is raining where he is. The rain reminds
the world of the folly of being over-serious,
one can never be bored when it's raining,
and hummingbirds never get wet.

Old Ernie Harrington had the knack
of pacing his jokes, or rather his joke. He'd wait
until he knew you wouldn't be able to remember
the punch line, then he'd tell the joke again.
I was just a kid and we would be driving
past a cemetery and he'd say how many dead people
do you figure there are in that cemetery, David,
and I'd know it was a joke and I'd try to remember
the punch line but would finally say I don't know
and he'd say they're all dead, and then he'd say
you often see a restaurant but you never see a
rest-your-uncle. And he used to win prizes for his
dahlias.
            During the thirties he used to listen
to Dick the Amateur Gardener's Radio Show. In fact
he belonged to the Dick the Amateur Gardener Fan Club.
One time he went to Toronto to attend a talk
being given by Dick the Amateur Gardener
and later he got in a discussion with Dick
and began bragging about how beautiful Hamilton was,
and Dick said well Toronto would be just as beautiful
if it had an escarpment running through the centre of town,
and Ernie said if you piled up all the garbage in Toronto
in the centre of town you'd have an escarpment.
He used to like to tell that story.

And he used to talk about his brother Eddie

who got killed in France in World War I. He would
start crying whenever he mentioned his name.
He said Eddie was a pacifist who went to war because
he didn't want to break his mother's heart by refusing.
Before going he confided in Ernie that he'd vowed to himself
never to fire his gun at another human being.
That's why he got killed in his first battle, said Ernie,
and the tears would start to fall. Ernie married
a widow with three children, and they had three children
of their own, and that is why I'm writing this poem,
he died yesterday and is going to be buried
next to his wife's first husband
with just enough room for her to be buried
between them when she dies.

# Country of the Open Heart

## I

When the phone rings in the middle of the night
the toes of angels curl like pigs' tails,
long-term vegetarians long for raw slabs of bacon
and a naked voice enters the head, a voice from the
mountains that encircle the lives of dreamers,
and the voice is as soft as the core of the heart,
the faithful molten centre of voluptuous art,
a voice so human the chips (with gravy) fall
into the polonnoise sauce of daily life
and the heart somersaults into silence
at the surprise eruption of its own inhumanity
and the murdered beauty of the loveliest life
on a Friday night in 1975 at the Cecil Hotel
in cold rainy downtown Vancouver with seven salesmen
sitting at a table heavy and wet with adjectival beer.
But talk shifted to colour and it became apparent
all seven were at least partially colourblind.
And the talk turned to aging and it became apparent
all seven had been born on the same day
and each was celebrating his fortieth birthday.

The phone rings in the middle of the night.
The dreamer's heart is wearing a transparent bikini.

## II

The dog stood on the bark, burning,
in the oceanic night of deliberate oil spills.
The dog picked up the pipe and puffed it,
the dog was discovered reading Pascal
and drowned in two inches of rainwater
while squirrels and cats refused to help
and his last thoughts were of you, tied
to a television antenna, your limbs

so long and white and leathery in the rain
and amid the thunder and lightning your voice:
"Don't forgive them, they know what they're doing."
From up there you saw the sea become as calm as a clam
as the murderous mob embarked for paradise
for their first return in three thousand years
but they found it had lost its rustic charm
and this kind of sentiment is an affliction
reminiscent of the kind of person who can fall
down a flight of stairs without spilling a drop
of his mind. "So this is paradise, eh?
Be a nice place if they ever get drunk
on the spirit of the age and punch holes in
the invisible wings of truck-driving dreamers,
cut down a few of those overbearing trees,
straighten out those crooked roads of genius."


### III

Hands up those with hairy armpits.
Your heart is being torn in twain
by the banks of the river of the transparent
self which has perfected the freedom to say
anything but what it really wants to say.
Whatever became of Catullus' yacht?
All energy comes from desire's reversal
said Venus to Adonis long ago
(of course Adonis really said it to Venus
but it doesn't scan) (another reversal)
and the human race has awakened and now
must reverse itself and fall asleep again —
the grapefruit tastes so wonderful
between mouthfuls of fresh lobster —
and the holy trees still long to resume
their impregnation of would-be tyrants
for whom time itself travels in reverse,
waves crashing out from barbaric shores
like radio signals from frantic planets,
shrinking into the past with vast intelligence
and the knowledge that nothing need be known,

crushed spiders becoming whole again
and shrinking into tiny eggs,
drowning in a sea of ordinary light,
apes drowning in a sea of butter,
lions and tigers in a tidal wave of cream,
giraffes saved by their long sweetheart necks.

The gibbons are butchering each other
at the far end of the jungle;
their hairy dead bodies like sleeping swamis
litter the beach between jungle and sea
of soured buttermilk. Fate hath a way
of providing such incredible spectacles,
and during the hostilities lobster
will not be available unless an unusually
adventurous gibbontrepreneur dares the trip
through the holocaust to the creamy constant shore.
No plans have been made to chronicle this war.

And the river that runs through the centre
of the jungle where peace-loving tribes
of gibbons toss grapefruit at each other
is stained with piss and grapefruit juice
and their fabulous music never ends
or just when you think it's about to end
a DC-10 crashes in downtown Toronto
and your doctor informs you a giant tapeworm
has formed a cave in the centre of your brain
with care, with attention to all the details,
with obvious permanence in mind,
and is sucking at the backs of your eyeballs
as if they were memory glands
lowing with spurts of optical milk aglow
in creation's instant midnight of typewriters.
And the reader's attention stretches lazily
at the centre of a hollowed-out modern romance
and he dreams of the carnage on the beach
or the hollowed-out centre of Toronto.

# IV

The heart hath a handle in hell
and holds in its lap a bowl of constant cream
that changes its poisonous savour with the changing
tides of fashion but the blood that flows
in all directions through time's hemispheres
has its own knowledge of ecstasy and terror
unrelated to such frivolous concerns:
thus in the sea, when tides are strongest,
the surface often shows its calmest face
and the agony of cruel crucifixion
lies behind the saint's beatific smile
as your writing, when it appears to be
pretending to reflect spiritual truth,
is merely moving through the nature of itself
like a snake awakening on a mild spring morning.

Everybody notices everything, but no one
who hath not a heart in hell's constant cream
can understand the breakdown of the world,
or the incessant cursing of the mind's unhappiness
in the surprise of the world's merriment.
An open heart is a joy entirely
and is enough to float a mighty thought
or a mighty fleet of little thoughts
for under its furry red jacket
the heart is a fierce little mole
that can burrow forever in any direction
and change its course with the lightest thought
— so light it can never touch itself
and its very existence can't be detected.
Welcome to the country of the open heart.
Virginia is for lovers. Hospitality spoken here.
Concerto for lover, flute and harp.
Once open never to be closed again.

# V

The rediscovery of paradise was billed
as the Canine Caper of the Century
and why not? The entire Pacific Ocean
is a Spanish onion and you've never
found it difficult to say where one ocean
begins the day with a hearty breakfast
and the other seldom fasts at all.
While the hounds of heaven guard hell's gates
and yelp and yowl with almost human glory
the ocean begins to throb with devotion,
the naïve saloonkeeper asks Mae West
to sing for him, you want your every song
to be pregnant with the ecstasy of the age
(for to sing is to enter the Western
Gates of Paradise where heavenly hounds
do shake the darling buds of Mae
if not the aging or even the aged)
and in the planetarium of heavenly pop bottles
a one-eyed lady sings a song about a total
eclipse of the sun and expresses sweet regret
that she and her lover would probably be dead
before the next one and you, uncharacteristically,
said: "Heck, the way I'm going I'll be lucky to see
Halley's Comet," and later your cousin Fred
while on a night flight from Vancouver to Toronto
noticed a vertical line in the sky —
on one side of the line the sky was dark
and on the other side light — and just then
the pilot announced the scientific name
for the phenomenon and described it as
"the line that separates night from day."
So on his next flight Fred stayed awake
deliberately all night long looking for that line
but it failed to appear, and having forgotten
the scientific name for that most essential
of all lines, he wrote a note to the pilot:
"What do you call the line
that separates night from day?"
and the pilot sent a note back saying

"I don't know what you're talking about."
— Just think of this story as a contribution
to the notion of contribution, an executioner
in a black hood full of inexpressible delights
singing a lullaby to himself while awaiting victims,
a chronicle of Empty Lives and civilized brutality
and the road to hell is paved with dead dogs
and maybe the occasional dead cat.

This is your Empty Lives report
for Monday, May 28 — but first
a word from the bottom of the open heart.
Howdy, strangers. Do you sometimes feel
Empty Lives passing through your Open Heart?
Not nice is it? Well, we have the answer.
Tell it to the Lord in prayer. This message
is from the Open Heart Pornography Co-op where you
can find the finest in new and used passion,
thoughtless people stomping on your tenderest memories,
rabble-rousing racists raving about recent betrayals,
and incestuous denials of wrongdoing in low places.
A ridge of Empty Lives is moving across
the Sechelt Peninsula bringing feelings of
depression and hopelessness to the area.
Record suicide rates have been reported
in Bay St. John and Two Lips County
— even these lines are about to commit suicide
to protest in advance their lack of readers
and their inability to continue on forever
in a universe of their own deconstruction
for it's impossible to imagine a time or place
when or where anything that exists didn't.
This problem comes from Incredible Woe
and what is your loneliness but the planet's?
And if you think this is pathetic
you should have seen the first draft!
You are watching a heart grown wild and strange,
a heart of suddenly inexplicable rhythmic patterns,
a heart of gradual basic coquetry sublime
and that heart is your sole possession
and don't think your friends don't admire

the calm detachment with which you observe
your heart's grotesque configurations,
for its attempts to protest its sufferings
and the cruelty of the age in which it lives
and its attempts to assert its lost glory
and its attempts to rebel against its fate
and achieve victory over that ever-popular
stand-up comedy team of Death and Death
are, at best, half-hearted.

## VI

The blood that was used to boil the skulls
flows in every conceivable direction
in the country of the open heart
where cats and dogs discuss the weather
and there are as many ways of fearing
death as there are of dying.
You may plunge forward courageously
into the madness of your life
but the sky is full of snakes
and you're paralyzed by theoretical
considerations of human freedom
for a snake is a long line of perfect verse,
there are no adjectives in heaven,
you don't know who to love and the open
heart is a spreading pool of boiling grease.

Fall away from sin and grief
for your mind is the heart of the land of your birth,
said the sea as it pounded away at transparent hearts
with the rhythms of sleazy 1950ish surrealism
and the heart is a flame the damned can love
with a desperate passion that vanishes with the world,
the question of doubt never coming to climax —
all over the world the sound of corks
popping and dust rising on country roads.
Is this folk music? Can a glass
of ordinary red blood be set to music?
There is nothing that cannot be planted

but thinking makes it grow, this wisdom,
the only wisdom worth living for,
the wisdom of the wind from the heart,
the wined wind that will never wind down,
the unwound heart, the wound-down heart,
and the heart that can never be wounded.

The autopsy showed a bottle of wine
had somehow lodged in your heart.
Probable cause of death: poor vintage.
Forever drawing back from that final drink,
civilization itself is the perfect epicurean.
You refused to drink to excess so your cousin Fred
bonked you with a bottle of Vichy water
(would you be annoyed if someone picked up
a raisin from the floor and dropped it in your
steaming plate of beef haiku and spinach?).

When a billion people start writing
someone is bound to write something like this.
He told you to count your blessings and try
to live one day at a time and you
set fire to yourself in the village square.


## VII

The heart is a power dam on that network
of thick black blood flowing in all directions
without motive, while the angels, their spread wings
invisible as music of the future, as energy
which lifts and lightens heaviest woe,
as the sadness of beautiful animals
and trees and discarded artifacts undreaming
in dim corners of the studied human earth,
likewise fly in all directions, magnetism as real
as a blackberry bush, knowing itself only to be
part of a music it will never hear.
A blood-boiled human skull sitting in the dump,
tourists indulging in silly arguments,
the skull's eyes empty as opal rings,

and the skull waddles away as cameras click,
flooding the future with unfocussed images,
and someone throws a beer bottle at the skull
and someone sticks a cigar butt in the blowhole
of a trapped whale and the skull turns with sudden
fear and runs smack into a wall of rock like a
romantic stuck in the middle of a modern romance
and before the tourists' dull cameras and sharp eyes
the skull transforms itself into a mountain goat
and scampers straight up to the first ledge,
glances down, then climbs straight up to the second
and the sun goes down and the moon comes up
and the tourists strip and start howling like gibbons
unburdened of humanity's impossible woe
by an extremely rare convergence of stars,
skull and mountain goat, dangerous
as a dream impossible to remember
in the open country of deathless art
where love occasionally travels in reverse
so that it starts sour and ends sweet
and becomes more and more intense till it suddenly
disappears like a butterfly unpinning itself
in the window of a Chinatown gift shop.

A tale told by the King of Burgundy
who owns all the whales in the Western Sea:
Three ugly nuns — perhaps the ugliest
in all Christendom — were walking along
the lonely road from Aix-en-Provence
when they were accosted by a strange creature,
half bear, half goat, who began
pestering them with terrible jokes about nuns.
"Why do they call them nuns? None better.
Haw haw haw," he bellowed, obnoxiously,
slapping them on their backs with all his might
and breathing foul bear breath in their faces.
Then, as if that weren't bad enough:
"Three nuns are sitting in the tub," he said.
"One says where's the soap? Second says
I don't know. Third says sure does.
Haw haw haw haw." Oh he was hawful!

And the nuns suddenly stripped off their habits
and showed they were really men in disguise,
robbers seeking safe passage to Marseilles,
and they abused that foul half-bear half-goat
mercilessly and left him half-dead in the road.

## VIII

A dog is barking in the Garden of Eden
where the swans and the blueberry honk and bloom,
vainglorious reality is covered with moth eggs
and time is an omelet ready to fold.
The animals on other continents
have perfected intricate patterns of war
but here the palm trees are amazed at their rapid
development of dreaded self-consciousness.
Imagine, if you will, a sad old palm tree
singing "Don't get around much any more"
accompanied by Blueberry Bush on tin whistle.
This is a song to sadden the gladdest heart
though it won't get you anywhere important. This
is modern romance at its best, a veritable sex killer's
vision of the annual picnic at the orphanage:
enough undiluted sperm to float a boatload of roses
along the River of Broken Hearts and Dreams
where each glistening drop of sparkling dew
is a perfect little human being
waiting to be wakened into bliss
or simply wakened by, for instance, a romantic
laser beam aimed at the tiny perfect opal
suspended in a pocket of tears at the centre of the
heart, the heart opening into the country of its birth,
a country overrun by angelic warlords
and swept daily by golden firestorms
proven by independent research agencies
using narrow-spectrum occurrence computers
to possess a malevolent form of intelligence
and a subtly childlike sense of humour.
The blackberry bush flowed in all directions.

Oh how fast these lines are running —
lines for filthy minds, written by a lonely
bar of soap melting in a pool of bath-tears.
One cannot claim authorship for a vague
intuition that if one continues reading / writing
something wonderful will happen.
You will receive a wonderful surprise.
That small tingling sensation will gradually grow
and your heart will begin to pound like butter
and you, my love, will turn into a blackberry bush
and your eyes will open and you will find
all as it was when your eyes were closed
for this is the country of the open eye
where Shelley's glaciers stare at you like snakes
and the sky with a sigh is about to defame your name
and nature ropes its way around your neck
like the tail of an unrecallable nightmare beast
whose grey flesh rolls like tidal bores
over rank after rank of transparent soldiers:
the Light Brigade, country of open sores.
For every day you make things, except for the days
you steal things, and every time you write a bad line
a cancer patient somewhere goes into remission
and every time you write a good line someone dies
and goes to heaven where every day
is like today. It must have been wonderful
to have lived in Tahiti before those gangs of Gauguins
came over the horizon like little lines of
brilliant verse. Everything was taken care of
though it would have been better if nature had put
a nice fresh fish inside each coconut.

The blackberry bush of naked nuns
is flooded with images of a mind peeled
like a skull in boiling blood, and a heart pure
and thoughtless as a dog's tongue panting
in the heat of a passing passion
and you shake the dog off your embarrassed leg
and scold it, saying: "You bad dog —
you don't see me carrying on like that,"

and you are astonished as the dog starts talking
in a California accent even though it's a Labrador
and it says: "When I heard that women were more
emotional than men I burst into tears."


## IX

When it comes to the end of its current tragedy
the human heart opens as calmly as a clam
and squirts you in the eye. When you come
to the end of a perfect night you'll find
a Sleeping Princess with tiny naked breasts
and tiny naked breaths and you say what the heck
and you kiss her and she wakes up screaming
and the cops come and arrest you.
The nice cop says he knows you from somewhere
and you cry because he reminds you of your dad.
In fact you're crying a lot these days.
You look at a falling leaf and cry.
You see a man walking down the street
with a violoncello and you cry. You know
you'll die without ever playing like Rostropovich.
You remember catching leaves as a child.

Night falls and the heart shudders in its sleep.
Someone has filled the teapot with gravy.
A cat named Buddy is crying at the back door.
He is not worried about the plight of the world.
He doesn't even care if I ever finish this stanza.
Or, if I do, if you do, my dainty monsters.

But at the death of the Queen of Burgundy
the hearts of many shuddered in the sweet
light of dawn. Oh the agony. Can she really
be gone? For the greatest fear is of the death
of the beloved — does the cut earth forgive the worm?
To experience love the wholeness of the heart
must be split as perfectly as a birch log
and tossed in the fire of poetic cliché.
*Thunk.* That's all it took! The more

you split a heart the greater it becomes
until all death is settled in the death of the self
which can never occur except in a moment of extreme
self-torture for at the moment of death
there is no moment — only the open heart
bursting with endless hypocritical laughter.
Natalia was alive and now she is not.
Natalia not? Never! Aye that's the knot.
Fear death? Fear this thought in the mind?
This heap of dumb onions is for death's dominion
and for children catching falling leaves
in wild waves of unforgettable nothingness.

Hark! The kitten is crying again.
It is cold and wet and hungry like everyone.
The one you love is reading these lines.
Giant globs of saltwater are purling down
his or her inevitably adjectival face.


## X

October mind in the sky, October
heart in the earth, the harvest is in
as it always is, and these humiliations
are porters of the sea and land
teasing you with hints about your fate
like the angel lady who lives in your soul
and continually tells you she will never leave
and turns all time into a supermarket
and all space into your own empty stomach.
The earth is a rotten pineapple crawling with
maggots. Smoke, like streams of strange music,
rises from all the little houses in the mountains
and destroys forever all your beloved lyricisms
and she looks at you from across the room
and later the room looks at you from across her,
mountains unmistakably lost forever unlike
certain mountains in certain books of childhood,
the childhood you see wherever you look.
Oh, her eyes were as buttery as burnt almonds

and the room was continually shifting gears
like that most wonderful song, "A Sports Car
on a Mountain Road." Something you didn't
want to sing or drive.
                          Alas, illuminating heavens,
the music rises from these little alpine dwellings
and the little dwellings in all the little centuries.
Her eyes split your heart in twain and burned
each half black as Plutonian mushrooms.
Her eyes destroyed all understanding
in a solitude of oranges and cherryblossoms
in the rainy English summer of 1594.
Her eyes were inverted nipples flooding
her brain with constant optical cream. Her eyes
were dying soldiers in an ancient war.
Her eyes were the hearts of unknown assassins.

But the radiant night has a humour of its own
which delights in destroying your noblest verse
and farts in your face as you lie dreaming
of eyes that remind you of the first pair of leaves
on the first branch of the first tree in Eden
and your heart pounding with wild surmise
and her eyes were perfect lovers fated
never to come together and never part.
Her eyes were planets of negative desire
in a world where poetry and poetry
can never part and never come together.


                    XI


The human heart delivers itself
in plain brown language,
the language of erotic goddesses
and gives itself to inexplicably
erotic monologues so monstrously dull
newspapers have to be invented
far from the broken eye of paradise
frightful in cold feet on a bare night
under stars as steadfast as romantic poets

and the seasons have their seasonings of which
the least intelligent are most knowledgeable.
But the illusion of the heart's loneliness
is as pitiable as the heart's subtle realization
that it will never be lonely again is glorious,
as the heart unfolds its banner of open sores
across moonlit landscapes and the first of an entire
season of falling stars falls softly on its flesh
and pearls pop out like beads of melting chocolate.


## XII

These words will embarrass me for the rest of my life
by reminding me of my memory's soft spots:
the hungry cat is crying. Reading is dreaming,
writing is waking up and John Keats is staring
at the face of a dying soldier, purple and green,
in the parking lot of the Banff Springs Hotel,
June afternoon, everyone gone except security guards,
the mountains giant pyramids in the sun,
and Keats points out a long silent freight train
skirting the base of a mountain away in the distance.
And death's breath carves another line of verse
while the pearl of great price opens like a nose
and squirts you in the face. Seventh Day Adventists
please read no further. All others please continue.
So there's Keats still complaining about Shelley
and the soldier in the last gasp of his agony
glimpses a great happiness at the end of a perfect
language with no grammar but that of the open heart.

The heart is easily bored and loves to read romantic
novels that will never be written. The heart holds
a hundred-gallon aquarium containing hundreds of tiny
heartfish nibbling on the green slime of former
obsessions, and spectacularly respects its assumption
of emotional imperialism. Friends, the heart is no masochist
although nothing hurts like a herd of hurt hearts
or so I've heard. And when day is done and the stars squirt
ketchup and Hollywood corpses sail across the sky like clouds

134

the heart becomes insane with incredible life:
country of terrible sunshine on shipwrecks,
country of naive folksingers and generous priestesses
where the streets run with golden phoenix secretions
and gondoliers regard the earth as a ductless gland,
language devolving from the mysterious inner cavities
like planetary systems from the sun. And the moon
bobs in an ocean of dirty dishwater of course.
So simple even a child could put it together.
And what a child hath put together let no god
prevent the environment from taking on a life
of its own for we're all in the same wooden horse.
Inevitably, the moon illuminates a charming channel
where talking cats confound romantic sailors
with limited intellectual resources by offering
inexpensive aphrodisiacs. One minute a cat starts talking
politics and the next you have a dog on your hands.

And blood flows in all directions. Oh look!
A nest full of baby ospreys. And a young photographer
in a long overcoat. Life I want more and more of you.
Each year I love you more and more.

The burning blackberry flows in all directions
out to the limits of time's supermarket
and civilization is more obsessed with beauty
than a quick look at the twentieth century would indicate
but no more than that elegant young photographer
about to be murdered by the Mafia in the east end
of Hamilton, Ontario, in 1951. Awake:
overcoats like that become more and more fashionable
as each generation is born less furry
and with less fury. Asleep: the loss of fur
necessitates the sort of intelligence capable
of inventing a long overcoat (the old
let's-pretend-the-statue-is-alive routine) (the
open overcoat exposing the music's genitalia).
You need another line here. That'll do.

# Acknowledgments

An earlier version of "Night of Endless Radiance" appeared in *Acts of the Imagination,* a special issue of *Cross Country Magazine,* along with two other long poems, one by Ken Norris and one by Jim Mele.

An earlier version of "Country of the Open Heart" was published in a limited edition by Longspoon Press in Edmonton in 1982.

"The Cow That Swam Lake Ontario" was performed by Hawaiian Howard and the Indoor Plants at a benefit for writing students on February 5, 1982, at David Thompson University Centre in Nelson, B.C. The performance featured Noel Hudson, Calvin Wharton and Dave Scanlan on lead, rhythm and bass guitars respectively, Rob Hardy on tenor saxophone, Dietmar Trommeshauser on drums, and David McFadden on voice and maracas. It was part of a program featuring readings and performances by Marian Engel, Fred Wah, Margaret Hollingsworth, Tom Wayman, and Greg Curnoe.

"The Cow That Swam Lake Ontario" and "Stormy January" were published together under the title *A Pair of Baby Lambs,* by The Front Press, Toronto, 1983.

"Adults at Play" appeared in *The Antigonish Review.*

"Adults at Play," "Bev and Dwight," "The Deer Hunter," "Dying Metaphors," "Letter to My Father," "Greaseball," "Thirty-four Lines about Horses," "Kitsilano Beach on a May Evening," "Secrets of the Universe," and "The Rat" appeared in *Three Stories and Ten Poems*, published by Identity Press in Toronto in 1982.

"Margaret Hollingsworth's Typewriter," and "Margaret Hollingsworth's Milk" appeared in *Canadian Literature.*

"The Bunny Farm" appeared in *Not Poetry.*

"Tibetan Mandala" and "Tibetan Monologue" appeared in *CVII.*

"Crossing Second Narrows Bridge in an Old Blue Morris Minor" and "Malcolm Lowry" appeared in *The Capilano Review.*

"The Seduction of Queen Elizabeth II" appeared in *Rampike.*

"The Armadillo" appeared in *Zest.*

"Canada/My Earliest Memory" appeared in *Mudpie.*

Some of these poems were staged by the Buddies in Bad Times Theatre Company under the title "Nirvana at Twilight" in Toronto in 1983.

The author would like to thank all the editors who took an interest in this material, and especially Dennis Lee and Ellen Seligman of McClelland and Stewart. Acknowledgments are due to the Canada Council and Ontario Arts Council, to the English departments of Simon Fraser University and the University of Western Ontario, to Stan Bevington of Coach House Press for his many kindnesses, his belief, and for allowing me free and unlimited use of his sophisticated Unix computer system, upon which the final draft of this book was composed, and to David N. Slocombe and Nelson Adams, both of whom often came to Stan's assistance in explaining the operation of the system.